𝔏uther's
SMALL DICTIONARY

𝔉rom 𝔄al to 𝔃ululand

Janet Letnes Martin
and
Suzann (Johnson) Nelson

CARAGANA PRESS

CARAGANA PRESS
BOX 396
HASTINGS, MN 55033

Copyright © 1999 by Janet Letnes Martin &
Suzann (Johnson) Nelson

Printed in the United States of America.

Published by Caragana Press
PO Box 396
Hastings, MN 55033

Library of Congress Catalog Card Number 99-96077

ISBN 1-886627-06-1

FIRST EDITION – Second Printing

Cover Design: Joe Gillaspie, Hastings, MN
Printer: Sentinel Printing, St. Cloud, MN

To Our Readers

Dear Fellow Lutherans, Friends, & Fans,

After publishing our award-winning book, *Growing Up Lutheran: What Does This Mean?*, we decided we needed to publish a Lutheran dictionary not only for Lutherans who for one reason or another had forgotten their memory work and their Confirmation vows, but also for those outside the fold who don't understand what makes Lutherans do the things they do and think the way they think.

For you Lutherans who didn't stray far from the church basement or the homeplace, this book is just plain common sense. For instance, you know that the definition of **Basic Necessities** in life is "having a roof, white food, a Bible, one change of clothes, a flashlight, a seed catalog, and relatives visiting on Sunday." Nothing more, and nothing less.

For those of you who strayed, turned, or moved to town and lost your bearings, roots, common sense, and Lutheran guilt, this book will bring you back down to earth where you know you belong.

For those of you who didn't grow up belonging to Trinity or First, or who didn't associate with anyone named Benson, Bolstad, or Berg, you're missing a lot in life. However, if you married a Lutheran and need to understand him or her, this book will teach you how to talk their talk and walk their walk. You know you will have arrived when you're in a Lutheran church basement and you can't tell — by the food or the conversation — if it's a funeral or a wedding doings because it all seems so normal.

This is most certainly true!

Janet Letnes Martin & Suzann (Johnson) Nelson

OTHER BOOKS published by Caragana Press:

- Cream Peas on Toast
- They Glorified Mary/We Glorified Rice
- They Had Stores/We Had Chores
- Is It Too Windy Back There, Then?
- Uffda, But Those Clip-ons Hurt, Then!
- Growing Up Lutheran

Aal 1. The place in Norway that many Haugeans left so they could go to America and quit folkdancing and start clearing land. 2. The abbreviation for a German Lutheran-based insurance group that is infiltrating the Scandinavian Lutherans and taking former Lutheran Brotherhood policyholders. This isn't such a big deal though because both AAL and LB give away napkins for use in church basements. (See **Hans Nielsen Hauge**.)

Absent One of the Lutheran plagues tempting, and occasionally affecting, Sunday School kids. There was no excuse for this — not even the Asiatic Flu of 1956.

Accent What most Norwegian Lutherans had, and what parsley did to a bowl of potato salad.

Accept One of the Lutheran virtues. No matter what it is, just accept it and get on with life, i.e., "snap outta it."

Accessorize A word only used by local newspapers to describe the bride's "going away" outfit, and by Lutherans during Holy Week as in, "My, how the Mrs. would doll up her Easter outfit accessorizing it with pop beads and matching earrings, a new marshmallow purse and matching shoes, new gloves and matching hat, and her good girdle."

Accompanist The goal of all Lutheran mothers, i.e., that their daughter (regardless of piano talent) might someday become an accompanist for Luther League, 4-H, and regional choral contests. (See **Piano.**)

Accountable Another Lutheran virtue, this word is used almost hourly by Lutheran pastors, mothers, Sunday School teachers, hymnal salesmen, etc.

Acting Up Another Lutheran plague afflicting the species from birth through high school which only manifests itself at church functions, when the minister is "wisiting" your house, or on the school bus.

Activities Lutheran activities are allowed at Bible Camp (off-key unbalanced bands, tether ball, and greased watermelon contests,) at Sunday School picnics (horseshoes, kittenball, or gunnysack and wheelbarrow races,) and at Luther League meetings before lunch (musical chairs, blowing marshmallows across the table, and Bible races.) Except for 4-H, any other activity not listed here is frivolous and best limited to lazy town kids.

Adoption The most modest (and Lutheran-approved) way to have children.

Adulteress (*Uffda!* See **Affection**.)

Advent A season during which purple and pink candles were allowed in the church even though they clashed with the new Red Hymnal.

Advice A commodity prevalent among older Lutherans which is freely offered, even if not sought, desired, nor accurate.

Affection One of those borderline words like adulteress. It should be explained, but not practiced.

Afterlife 1. A longterm goal that dictates hourly behavior from cradle to grave. 2. A place from which grandparents and angels watch children's behavior and safety to the detriment of a Lutheran teen's full social life. 3. A place that is up or down, and if a Lutheran drinks, it is down.

Agnus Dei Latin spelling of the name, Agnes Day, the organist at St. Petri Lutheran Church.

Air This word has many uses in the Lutheran lexicon and vocabulary. It can be something Bach does on a G-string, it can be musty in a church basement, it can be lacking at a tent meeting, and a Swedish pastor can be full of it.

Air-Dry A method of getting church basement dishes done in a jiffy, but never utilized in a Lutheran Church Basement kitchen.

Aisle A place inside the upstairs of the church where scared Confirmands line up for Public Questioning, where nervous brides trip and faint, where self-conscious men button up their suitcoat on the way to the altar with the offering plates, and a place ruled by the head usher. (Do not confuse aisle cloth with oil cloth.)

All-Nighter A temptation that arises the last night at Bible Camp, but is closely monitored by strict counselors who were never young; what liberal arts majors at Lutheran colleges pull the night before a term paper is due during the freshman quarter in which they learned to play '500'; and what a graduating seminarian suffers through the night before his orals.

All Out 1. A phenomenon that never happens to the supply of food at a Lutheran Church gathering, but does happen to the workers if they wear the wrong shoes. 2. The pace at which one begins buttering the buns when an event is about to start.

Alpha and Omega Sort of the baptism and funeral of the Christian world; a cradle-to-grave span symbolized by the end view of a picnic table over a horseshoe.

Alto A lazy soprano.

Alumni A word always preceded by "faithful" as in "Concordia's faithful alumni would prefer that square-dancing be called square-gaming."

Amount A significant Lutheran word when applied to offering, as in "What amount did we take in?" and when applied to children, as in "She'll never amount to anything."

Anchor 1. A kind of cross used by early Christians in the catacombs. 2. The part of the boat that rebel Lutheran boys like to lose when rowing their new girlfriends at Bible Camp.

Anniversary 1. Milestones in family life (the 25th or Silver is the most important), and in church life (the 100th or Centennial is the most important). 2. The only event at which a silver service set is used at church. (See **Silvers**.)

5

Annual 1. One of the means Lutherans use to keep things in order such as the Annual Meeting (which can get disorderly), Annual *Lutefisk* Supper, Annual Sunday School Picnic, and Annual Harvest Bazaar. 2. A type of flower planted by floozy women who have too much time on their hands. (See **Order**.)

Antiphonal Readings What all 14-year-old Lutheran boys (and the few Lutheran girls who were tone-deaf) were expected to do at the Annual Sunday School Christmas Program.

Apocalypse Has something to do with the 'Book of Revelation,' and with relighting the pilot light in the church kitchen stove.

Apron A necessary piece of clothing that comes in six basic styles for six basic types of events in the Lutheran Church Basement (See 'Growing Up Lutheran,' page 141.) A positive item unless it has the word "strings" attached and then it is negative, as in "He's such a sissy. He's still tied to his mother's apron strings." This is a utilitarian garment that can be used to gather eggs and windfall apples and, if made of canvas, it is a man's garment for transporting nails or holding change at the County Fair admission gate.

Attendance Pins A goal of a Lutheran child and

his family is to have the longest ladder of bars under the attendance pin signifying ten to twelve years of perfect Sunday School attendance.

Augsburg College A little Lutheran haven in the heart of sin city that produces graduates who make their living writing Lutheran dictionaries and books about peas, Catholics, and hotflashes.

Augsburg Publishing House The Library of Congress of Lutheran publications from tracts to Sunday School materials to nice books to choral music. One of the few places where a Lutheran can spend money guilt-free, right up there with Watkins, Stanley Home Products, and the feed store.

Auxiliary A branch of the Lutheran hierarchy that usually does the grunt work, i.e., the Ladies Aid.

Average What all Lutheran children are.

Awkward What sixth-grade Lutheran girls and ninth-grade Lutheran boys are. How a Scandinavian-Lutheran feels at a funeral when talking to the spouse of the deceased.

𝐵...

Babel The sound coming from immigrants when Norwegians from many different valleys were assembled; usually heard at a national *bygdelag* gathering.

Backbite Not a formation of the mouth and jaw like an underbite, but an evil against thy neighbors that Martin Luther warned about that rates right up there with "belie" and "betray."

Backbone Those who are the main support of a Lutheran organization such as the President of the Ladies Aid, the senior citizens with money and time on their hands, the blond in Luther League who plays flute and doesn't giggle in front of a group, the Founders of the Cemetery Association, etc.

Backfire What Jerald Jensrud's pickup did when he parked for the Luther League hayride, and what happened to Klara Klepperud when she spread gossip about Donna Christianson's husband. (See **Gossip**.)

Balcony A place where Lutheran boys sit during Sunday Services to defy authority, where bats congregate in country churches, and where new Red Hymnals are found in the Green Hymnal era.

Banquet The final thing a congregation could do for its youth before turning them out into the wide, wild world, as in "Ya, well, s'pose, then, we'll have to have a senior banquet before we send them on their way." (An event that students didn't want to attend, and parents didn't want to organize, but it had always been done before, i.e., a necessary Lutheran evil.)

Bare Bones A colorless term used by the Cemetery Association to describe both its budget and the items that Lars Larson dug up with the backhoe.

Baritone 1. A male singer who can't quite hit the bottom notes. 2. A huge golden instrument that occasionally showed up at a Bible Camp band to make pretty music with six flutes, fourteen clarinets, and one trumpet.

Barley An itchy grain used by Lutheran women to bake bread, and by Catholic men to make malt liquor.

Bars 1. The most basic of Lutheran foods which, when served with egg coffee in a church basement, does for the body what the wafer and wine does upstairs for the soul. 2. In the Catholic Church this word refers to main street establishments where real Lutherans are never found, i.e., a place where Catholics can go to get away from the Lutherans.

Basic Necessities For Lutherans these included a roof, white food, a Bible, one change of clothes, a seed catalog, a flashlight, and relatives visiting on Sunday.

Basket Social What young adult Lutherans did before there were liturgical dance practices.

Baskets for the Poor Brown paper bags packed with food by church women and distributed at Christmas by the sheriff to people with no names, but with lots of kids.

Bass 1. A tenor who is confirmed and shaves. 2. A Lutheran fish that pastors and farmers like to catch on vacation, but it isn't pronounced like the singer.

Basting An activity done to turkeys on Thanksgiving and to dresses before Easter.

Batchin' It What Torvald was doing when his wife was at the Synod Conference in Willmar. From the base word, "bachelor."

Bathing Cap A white hollow rubber ball with a snap-strap that Lutheran mothers forced their daughters to pack for Bible Camp. It was said to prevent ear infections, but proven to prevent camp boyfriends.

Bath Water A reusable resource found in galvanized tubs in Lutheran kitchens on Saturday nights, and on top of the pansies on Sunday morning after checking that the baby wasn't thrown out with it.

Bazaar A town word that means Mission Festival.

Bear/Bore (p.t.) 1. Something like crosses and burdens you shoulder for others when you don't have enough guilt already. 2. The act of producing fruit or children. 3. The force of buckling down, as in "Sylvia bore a child out of wedlock and her poor mother bore this burden to her grave and so then Sylvia had to finally bear down and get a job (raising boars) to support her child and bear her own burdens. She became a bore!"

Beastly Cold The temperature at which rural church services could be canceled, pronounced "beastly *kaldt*" in Norwegian-American homes.

Becoming Among Lutherans this word is usually used to describe a new dress or a pair of glasses as in, "My, it's so becoming to her," rather than to describe a state of being. The exception is when describing a potential seminarian, as in "He's thinking about becoming a minister."

Bedding A common Lutheran noun used to describe blankets in the house, straw in the barn, and compost on the flowers. Never used as a Lutheran verb.

Beeswax A politically-correct Lutheran way to say "business," as in "It's none of your beeswax."

Beet Pickles The maroon variety of pickles that stains organdy aprons and turns scalloped potatoes a pinkish color like the hue of a slop-pail full of Pepto-Bismol or Stanley Glass Cleaner.

Begat A word which was never fully explained as meaning "fathered." A Biblical way of saying "bun in the oven." A prefix and suffix to unpronounceable names, such as "Habakkuk begat Ishmael who begat Hosea who begat Janet, etc." A word which preceded long lists of Old Testament names and scared the bejeebers out of little Lutherans when they were asked to read these passages out loud in Sunday School. (See **Produce**.)

Behalf 1. This is always preceded by "on," and followed by "of," and used to politely say that a Lutheran hotshot decided not to show up at a do-ings, as in "On behalf of the bishop, I bring you greetings." 2. It doesn't mean 50-50 or something being halved.

Behave One of the four parental commandments: Behave, Act Decent, Don't Get Your Name in the Newspaper, and Turn Out.

Benediction A word that Lutherans both struggle with and look forward to. Pastors say they are going to "pronounce" it, but they never do. Instead, they recite some phrases. The "Omega" of the church service, and a signal that it is finally time to go to the bathroom. (See **Alpha and Omega**.)

Bethany Grill A Christian-oriented *lefse* griddle frequently given by the groom's parents to the newlyweds to ensure tradition while simulta-neously supporting a Bible School in Minnesota and its mission work.

Bias 1. Something old Lutherans have against Catholics, and old Norwegians have against

Swedes. 2. A cloth tape used to lengthen hand-me-down dresses. 3. A way to cut neckties and kerchiefs, but not corduroy.

Bingo 1. A game Catholics play to raise money for pagan babies. 2. A common name for black-colored Lutheran dogs.

Birthday Bank A plastic church with a slot in the roof where Lutheran kids put pennies on the Sunday nearest their birthday, one penny for each year of life.

Birthday Suit A lack of apparel "donned" by heathens near the mission fields and by streakers at Luther College.

Black and White 1. The colors of church anniversary and Bible Camp photos. 2. A Lutheran way of viewing things. 3. A tongue-in-cheek reference to police cars and nuns.

Bleach What Lutheran farm women do to the dishtowels, what Methodist town women who bowl do to their hair, and what we all want to do to our sins, i.e., bleach them white as snow.

Blend 1. A smooth way to obscure flaws. For example, mixing mayo into meaty deadspreads for funeral buns. 2. Putting together mixed things, i.e., what the Sunday School choir director hopes the children's voices will eventually do. (Only in the most dire circumstances will Lutherans do this to families.) (See **Deadspreads**.)

Blessings These usually come in abundance. Everything we have and see is one of these, including snakes and dust. We try to be thankful for them all, without ceasing.

Bloodclots These usually occur in Lutheran legs of the church organist, or in men who wear sock garters. One of the three legitimate excuses for "not serving." (See **Death** and **Hip Fractures**.)

Blow Over A Lutheran way of saying "This, too, shall pass." It usually refers to newfangled ideas for hymnals, or to snits among circle leaders.

Bluing A necessary chemical mixture procured and used by Lutheran women for church basement dishtowels, bed sheets, and hair color. It is okay to spend money on this because the towels will get so white, it will guarantee that you will be asked to wash the towels again.

Borneo A place overseas where missionaries go "to do outreach" but no one else ever visits, and where birthday bank pennies are sent to get pencils and tablets for kids who can't write.

Bosom A part of the body that we sing about but never talk about.

Boutonniere A male accoutrement as vital to Lutheran male church ushers as aprons are to Lutheran Church Basement Women (See **Apron**.) It is unclear how this French word crept into Scandinavian and German Lutheran vocabularies when "flower" is easier to say and spell, but it may stem from a kind of communion wine purchased on sale when the Mogan David was all gone.

Bouquet A vital Lutheran decoration for important church functions and, while it is mandated that the bride toss her bouquet, the groom must not toss his cookies.

Bowl A Lutheran noun; a Catholic verb.

Bratwurst The German Lutheran term for the Scandinavian Lutheran word, "wiener." Both words can be shortened and applied to mean boys, i.e., "brats and weenies!"

Brooch A fancy pin worn center-collar by the Founders of the Ladies Aid and pronounced "broach," but that's what we do with subjects.

Brotherhood A nice-sounding word to describe Christian men who either meet Monday nights and forget their rubbers at church, or who sell insurance.

Brownie Camera A box camera capable of taking only black and white pictures during daylight, and brought to Bible Camp to capture fond memories of counselors, bell towers, visiting missionaries, plus six shots of the lake.

Bruises What you cut out of windfalls when you bring an apple pie to the Mission Festival.

Buck 1. A white shoe that male Confirmands wore to match their gowns. 2. What you put in the offering when it is "free will." 3. The reason Torkel Tollefson was late for the Annual *Lutefisk* Supper in November '58; "He was home dressing his buck."

Buddy System A safety process at Bible Camp during which Lutherans could hold hands without being teased. (See **Holding Hands**.)

Budget Something that everyone talks about but no one understands, and every congregation needs but none ever follows. A synonym for "shortfall."

Bulletin A folded piece of paper that invites readers to prayerfully consider things. It can also be used as a roadmap through the Worship Service, or to stifle hotflashes during services. A vital statistics

18

weekly column that announces illnesses, marriages, births, and the pastor's upcoming two-day "leave."

Bulova The preferred brand of watch given by parents in the 50s and 60s to the successful Confirmand thereby ensuring that he or she would be home on time now that he or she could legitimately date Lutherans of the opposite sex who were also confirmed and had watches.

Bulwark 1. Something that never fails. 2. What oxen did with plows. 3. A word in the Lutheran fight song, 'A Mighty Fortress,' which was memorized and sung *forte* and with gusto, but never understood. Apparently something was lost in the translation from Martin. (See **Never-Failing**.)

Bunch of Hoodlums A term to describe the boys who defy authority by sitting in the balcony and by letting their pickups backfire outside the church.

Burdens What guilt-obsessed Lutherans bear for one another even on good days, and what old folks don't want to become to their children in old age.

Burning Bush 1. How Mavis Lundstrom described Ruby Dybdal's ratted beehive after Ruby overdosed on henna rinse for Easter Sunday. 2. What happened at the Severud's farm on August 30 when Sven Ole was so preoccupied with thoughts of grasshoppers that he didn't notice that the over-shoe section of the Sears-Roebuck Catalog blew out of the burning barrel and right into the Mrs.'s lilacs and peonies.

Burning the Mortgage A minor church festival that often occurred 25 years after a church was built if, of course, the members had faithfully tithed, and if the church hadn't burned up before the mortgage did.

Bustline A word only used in Home Ec class, never in the home or at church. (See also **Bosom**.)

Butcher 1. The man at a shop in town who makes the *bratwurst* for the *Kraut* Suppers at the German Lutheran Church. 2. A verb for what the farmer's wife does to the chickens on Saturday. (See **Kraut Suppers**.)

Butter A yellow substance than can never be thick enough or sweet enough or available enough for true Lutherans. The perfect accompaniment to, and camouflage for, white foods. Never used on coffee, dill pickles, or Jell-O, but allowable and often desirable on any other Lutheran food.

C...

Cabinet Wooden storage units of which there are never enough. Although they are identical in size, substance and purpose, they are called "cabinets" if they are located in the pastor's office, and "cupboards" if they are in the kitchen.

Cakepan Containers that are so precious to their owners that they mark their initials on them with red fingernail polish, and then they forget to take them home from church. When a surplus of these precious but forgotten pans builds up in the kitchen it is noted in the bulletin.

Cakewalk An allowable Lutheran circle game if participation is limited to once a year. For example, you can "go on the cakewalk" at the church Mission Festival as long as you didn't do it at the school carnival. If you already did it at school, that's enough foolishness for one year and if — heaven, help you — you won a cake already at the school

cakewalk, then for cryin' out loud it's for sure someone else's turn to be lucky.

California A place far away, probably overseas,
where people are different.

Call/Called (p.t.) This is a concept that is both
easy and hard to understand. Every Lutheran
woman knows what it means "to be called to serve."
It means that Sivert Paulson finally passed on and
the funeral will be big. On the other hand, select
Lutheran men have also been "called to serve," but
no one really knows what that means, how the
message is delivered, or who hears it. We only
know that this kind of "calling to serve" is more
important than bringing bars to a funeral.

Cancan In the Lutheran world, the "cancan" is
not a dance but rather a 50-yard slip made of netting and ribbon that Alice Long popularized on the
Lawrence Welk show which Lutheran girls from
the Midwest then donned under flarey skirts to
make a fashion and social statement, i.e., "Yes, we
have TV now." Twenty yards fit under the Sunday
School table and under Confirmation gowns, but
50-yarders made Confirmations gowns look like a
pyramid formed over a hula hoop. (See also **Pantaloons** and **Petticoat**.)

Candelabra The word used for a normal candleholder if it's going to be used on the altar or at a wedding. Otherwise, it's just a plain candleholder. A rose by any other name . . . .

Canon A set of mysterious religious books, or a song in D by Pachelbel not to be misspelled "cannon" which is a big metal thing by the soldiers' graves that Lutheran kids crawl on when their moms are doing dishes in the basement and their dads are folding bulletins.

Cantata A religious musical work that must have originated in Hatton, ND even though the word isn't Norwegian. Heavier than a hymn, but not as showy as an opera, it is performed annually and never has enough men participating.

Car Washes A fundraising activity used by kids in town churches so they could "go ye forth" to youth conventions in various sin cities throughout the nation with other Lutheran youth who spent the Spring washing cars in other states. The most successful car washes were held the Saturday before Easter at churches where the roads were gravel.

Carbo-Salve A good Christian gift for the janitor, Willie Bolstad, that gives a homemade mustard poultice a run for its money.

Carol 1. Familiar Christmas tunes that everyone knew the first verse to, and a few foreign ones, like 'Good King Wenceslas' and 'Wind Through the Olive Trees,' that didn't make sense and no one liked. 2. The name of a Lutheran girl born in December who usually had the middle name of Jean.

Caroling A sanctioned winter evening activity for Lutheran junior high kids, regardless of singing ability or voice change, who stand half in and half out of the doorway, get some fruitcake, shake a frail hand, and end with the secular song, 'We Wish You A Merry Christmas.'

Carpenter Even though this was the occupation of our Lord, most Lutheran men made excuses when this kind of work had to be done at church even though 80 percent of them had one of these pencils above their ears six days a week.

Casserole High church word for "hotdish."

Celebrate An activity requiring emotion that is often talked about, but rarely carried out at Lutheran Churches.

Cemetery High church word for "graveyard."

Cemetery Board Member One of the highest

positions in the Lutheran Church hierarchy.

Centennial A celebration of a Lutheran Congregation's 100th year that necessitates the sprucing up of the grounds, the repainting of the basement, the design and sale of ornamental hanging plates, the writing and publication of a book which emphasizes the founders and stained glass window donors, and the erection of a new sign at the crossroads to be painted — with just a touch of *rosemaling* —by Mrs. Halvor Erickson.

Center of Attention What no Lutheran kid could become even though he/she was all spruced up and had his/her memory work all done.

Chalkboard A high church word for a blackboard which was green anyway.

Chalktalk A colorful disguised sermon given by talented itinerant preachers to lure families to Midweek Services.

Charm 1. A noun for bracelets worn to Luther League that were anything but charming. 2. A verb that describes what heathens did to snakes before the missionaries came, or one that implies affection, as in "Sven Nestegaard charmed his way into Audrey Amundson's heart." 3. An adjective to describe preschool choir kids.

Charitable Construction A term that has changed meaning over the years. Formerly these were words that had to be memorized to get through Confirmation. Now the phrase refers to Habitat for Humanity.

Charter Member The steadfast pillars of the local society who, for one reason or another, sacrificed something to start a new church, synod, or college, and whose descendents unto the third or fourth generations thought that this special status had privileges that trickled down to them. (See **Pillar**.)

Chastity A Lutheran virtue to be sought and maintained even though it was never explained so one never knew if one had reached it.

Chewing Gum A textured nodule with the elasticity and pliability of Sunday School clay found under Lutheran pews, serving tables, and little red chairs.

Chill An icy feeling emanating from Mrs. Snustad's pew when a baby over two months old was baptized.

Chilly An excuse used by post-menopausal women to get out of Fall cleaning at church.

China 1. The best dishes in the church basement

only used for weddings, silvers and funerals of people who pledged a lot and made good on it. 2. A place where missionaries went in the 30s and 40s to preach the gospel in a language they couldn't speak.

Choir Angels-in-training. The only group of Lutherans who are allowed to: a) express emotion — even though it's not their own, but the composer's, and b) wear robes like the pastor which automatically puts them closer to heaven, and ensures that they won't stand out — even though individual voices might.

Choral Reading Group A dumping ground for kids who can't sing. A boring, but equitable, experience for junior high kids who can't carry a tune or whose voices are changing, but need to memorize and perform something in 8th grade prior to starting Confirmation classes. A performing group that brings forth accolades from elderly Lutheran women who can still hear, but who never talk to youth otherwise.

Chore Boy Not a boy at all, but a gold-colored scrubber found by the church basement sink and used to get baked-on meatballs out of pans. When new, they are fancied up with spoons, measuring cups, and other things and used as corsages at bridal showers. (See **Nylons**.)

Chorsing (Pronounced "Shor-sing.") This has nothing to do with "chorus singing," but explains, instead, why Einar Berulfson was late to services and smelled a little.

Christen A Catholic word for "baptize."

Christmas Cards 1. An expenditure that the Mr. finds unnecessary, and the Mrs. finds extremely important. Even though she hates to write them, she feels that she must. She hates to send them, but loves to receive them. She plans to cut down on the number she sends, but never does until people die and then she remembers their families with a card so the dead person could just as well have lived. 2. A decoration for the top of the piano which tips over and is a nuisance, but yet, having a good number of them on the piano is a modest way to indicate social status.

Chunky Pickles More for show and table color than nutrition and flavor, these tasteless morsels fill the pickle dish quickly, and even though no one eats them, no one can say, "They didn't even serve pickles." (See also **Pickles** and **Relish**.)

Church Basement Poles Twirling around these in flarey skirts was as close as Lutheran girls ever got to dancing. (See also **Pillar**.)

Church Key 1. A missing item that Lutherans would use to lock and open the church if it were necessary. 2. A Catholic bottle opener.

Circumcision Something too painful to discuss, but okay to read about in the Bible.

Cistern A holding tank for water under the church pump; not related to Brethren.

Clapping Out Loud in Church A post-Red Hymnal pagan activity borrowed from boisterous, emotion-displaying, non-Lutheran sects, and introduced into mainstream Lutheranism simultaneously with the advent of drums and guitars in church and with dancing at Lutheran college campuses.

Clasp 1. As a verb, what Holy Rollers do with their hands. 2. As a noun, what Lutheran girls wear in their hair, and what Lutheran women have on the sides of their good girdles.

Classes There are four classes in the Lutheran Church and they have nothing to do with social status, but rather with age and learning: Sunday School classes, Confirmation classes, young adult classes, and adult classes.

Clean Another Lutheran virtue which can be used

to describe how everything should be. (The main preoccupation of Lutheran women is to clean.)

Cleanse One of the highest priorities of Lutheran Church Basement Women. It can apply to everything from soles to souls.

Clear Fingernail Polish 1. A frivolous adornment applied by Lutheran mothers of the bride, worn for one day, once per daughter. (If she gets married again, there's no clear fingernail polish bottle coming out!) 2. A powerful agent to stop runs in nylons which, if applied when the nylons are on, will remove the outer layer of the skin as well.

Cleats Miniature versions of flattened horseshoes that are nailed under penny loafers worn by town boys and under boots worn by cowboys that are designed to intimidate wholesome farm boys, attract the opposite sex of any faith, and announce their presence.

Clerical Collar A piece of clothing worn by pastors which, throughout the years, has changed its shape from a frilly, daisy style to a bland Nehru style worn to warn others that it is time to behave and act decent. Under a black gown it commands full respect; under a black shirt, almost full respect; under a brown shirt, respect; and under a light blue shirt, least respect.

Clip-Ons 1. A kind of earring worn by Lutheran women who have no desire to add more holes to their heads, but still want something to match their popbeads. 2. A kind of necktie worn by lazy or uncoordinated Lutheran men.

Clock-watcher Someone like Emil who wants to get to church 40 minutes early so he can be assured he will get his regular pew.

Closure A word Lutherans use to describe different kinds of cupboard or door latches, and television reporters overuse to describe the end of grief.

Clothing Drive A charitable excuse for finally throwing something away.

Club A word to describe where loose people hung out. (The exceptions are the Sunshine Club and 4-H Clubs.)

Clumsy A bad word to describe a kitchen worker who drops a cup, or an usher who bangs folding chairs.

Cobwebs The bane of Lutheran Church Basement Women rating right above teenage pregnancy and dangly red earrings.

Cocoa The preferred beverage of rural Luther Leaguers. Town Leaguers called it "hot chocolate." (Most liked it with marshmallows on top. Town kids had miniature ones, and farm kids used the big globby ones or whatever else was handy.)

Coffee Although not mentioned in the Bible, this liquid sustains Lutheran adults and congregational life. The thickness and flavor varies from synod to synod, but it is a well-accepted fact that Lutheran egg coffee reigns supreme.

Coffin Just like a big-sized immigrant trunk to transport precious cargo from one place to another, some were fancier than others.

Coin 1. As a noun, what Sunday School girls tied in the corner of their hankies for offering. 2. As a verb, what pastors do to phrases when their sermons are dragging.

Colicky An excuse word to describe crying Lutheran babies in churches with no cryroom.

Collect 1. A part of the Lutheran Service where nothing is collected. 2. What Curtie Mortensen, the newspaper boy, went door-to-door to do every Friday after school.

Collection A part of the Lutheran Service where

<u>something is collected</u> (or "taken up.")

Combine 1. As a verb, in a bad year what the Sunday School superintendent has to do with classes when there aren't enough teachers. 2. As a noun, in a good year what the farmers use to thresh the wheat.

Comfortable What kitchen workers' shoes should be, but the opposite of how a Lutheran should feel in church. Neckties, good girdles, and fire and brimstone sermons have been sanctioned by church hierarchy as appropriate ways to provoke a lack of comfort.

Commandment While Lutherans were only required to memorize ten of these and their meanings, Lutheran kids were required to live and follow 7000-8000 of them, such as "Thou shalt not waste water; Thou shalt not call long-distance in the middle of the day; Thou shalt not touch the electric fence, etc."

Common 1. A kind of cup used by Episcopalians. 2. A complimentary word to describe the new pastor's wife, "Oh, she's so common."

Common Sense A principle guiding all Lutheran behavior as in, "If you don't want to get killed in a car accident, don't ride in cars."

Commune 1. What Lutherans do at the altar. 2. Where hippies who went bad at Lutheran colleges went to live.

Compact 1. A kind of car that can squeeze in the pastor's designated parking space. 2. Mrs. Borg's powder holder in her purse. 3. How you want to pack the clothing drive boxes.

Company on Sunday Night A rural Lutheran activity that occurred weekly prior to the advent of television wherein one Lutheran family "wisited" another either out of boredom or habit in order to eat leftovers, discuss the sermon, and wind down before gearing up for another six days of work.

Contemporary A fancy Lutheran word for a Holy Roller Service (that not even kids like) at which Bible Camp songs are sung on Sunday mornings during worship as a way to reach out to attention-deficit Lutheran teens who might turn Holy Roller otherwise.

Controversy A colorful event created when a faction of traditionally opinionless Scandinavian Lutherans decide that hymnals don't have to be black, basements don't have to be mint green, and nurseries don't have to be buttercup yellow.

Corn Relish An inedible pickled vegetable designed to provide color and the appearance of plenty. Something no one "relishes" eating. (See also **Chunky Pickles**.)

Cornerstone A brick with a year on it that the building committee stood by for a photo. Contains secrets of the committee's meetings that won't be opened until all members and their direct descendents are dead.

Corset A full-body-torture-undergarment for a full-bodied Lutheran woman which combines the functions of a good girdle and a bra, but only requires one expenditure (at twice the cost) designed to make her suffer like a real Christian should. The word probably originated with the Norwegian word "*korset*" which is pronounced the same but means "the cross" and embodies the word "suffering." During the 60s, as Lutheran college kids encouraged their parents to "Hang Loose," many Lutheran mothers took this to heart. Corsets have declined in popularity ever since.

Cost The criteria by which all church kitchen purchases, and all Luther League activities, are judged.

Covet Thy Neighbor's Ox This was the "Thou Shalt Not . . . ." commandment that Lutherans knew they were least likely to break. (See also **Ox**.)

Cradle Roll A framed list of babies' names that hung in the church basement, but no one knew why — even when they were on the list.

Crank A word to describe a pastor from the old school, and a way to start the Model T after services.

Creation In religious terms, the "Alpha" event of church life which occurred in six days but could have been accomplished sooner if God had left out the snakes, dust, and chopped liver. In common terms, a word to describe a new 4-H Revue dress, i.e., "My, My. That's quite a polka dot creation." (See **Alpha and Omega**.)

Crochet A self-rewarding activity that kept Lutheran women's thoughts pure, their fingers nimble, and the bazaar cashbox full.

Croquet A family-oriented Sunday afternoon

game that is played outside, and even though they already know their colors and have developed some hand-eye coordination, it still challenges 50-year-old men.

Crown 1. As a noun, a millinery number for wisemen, or an awful item made of thorns. 2. As a verb, what Lutheran parents might do to children as in, "If you giggle one more time at the filmstrips of the heathens, I'll just crown you."

Cup and Saucer A companion set that became incompatible at "Silvers". As Myrtle Nelson, who was pouring at Ole and Anna Swenson's doings, said to Hjalmer Peterson, "Just the cup. Not the saucer." (See **Pour** and **Silvers**.)

Current 1. Electricity 2. Up-to-date. (See **Gossip**.)

D...

Daily A kind of bread Lutherans pray for; could have been either dark or white.

Dairy The main occupation of Lutherans in Wisconsin who like to get outside each morning to "smell the dairy air."

Damnation Eternal punishment, not a country.

Damper 1. What rain can put on the Annual Sunday School Picnic. 2. What Howard forgot to open on the woodstove, and the resulting soot on the windows made Easter Services seem just like the Good Friday Noon Service.

Dancing Pagan behavior that leads to premature motherhood and a ruined reputation. (See **Sin**.)

Dark 1. A good Lutheran color for clothes and cars. 2. One of two kinds of bread or chicken meat; the other was white.

Darn A bad word which describes a boring, yet necessary, thing done to Lutheran socks.

Darts A game Lutheran boys played in "romper" rooms, and a seam in a homemade dress that Lutheran girls learned to press the right way. (In town, the rooms the boys played in were called "rumpus" rooms. S'pose they were right, then.)

Dash 1. A Biblical word meaning "smite" or "crush." 2. A Lutheran word meaning, "Get outta here, pronto!" 3. A key measurement in a recipe. 4. The part of a car where Catholics kept St. Christopher (who got demoted and kicked off the dash a few years ago, and is now making a comeback.)

Dating What Lutheran boys and girls can do (with other confirmed Lutherans) when they are confirmed.

Deaconess 1. The Missouri Synod's answer to ordaining women. 2. A nun with a calling. (Some more nun than calling.)

Deadspreads The stuff put on funeral buns: minced ham on white, egg salad on wheat, and Cheese Whiz and olives on rye cut on the diagonal. These concoctions put on open-faced sandwiches were also served at weddings and other doings besides funerals, but then they were just called sandwiches.

Death One of the three legitimate excuses for "not serving." (See **Blood Clots** and **Hip Fractures**.)

Debt 1. The same as "sin" or "trespass," except when talking about hunting. 2. Someone with a lot of this is probably "on Relief." 3. How Norwegian-American Lutherans pronounce "death."

Decent A good, solid adjective to describe a good, solid Lutheran kid.

Dedicate Lutheran congregations dedicate everything from whole lives and buildings to new hymnals, tract racks, and new kitchen mixers.

Delegates Lutherans who are versed in the scriptures, synodical differences, and social issues, and who are trusted by the congregation. They are not afraid to speak up if pressed on an issue, not afraid to drive in traffic, and they own a car big enough to transport other delegates.

Depression Depression, as in "The Depression" is a Lutheran word; depression, as in "mental state," is not.

Deserving This is a good/bad Lutheran word. When something good happens, it evokes all sorts of guilt because somewhere, somehow, someone else doesn't have it so good, and therefore your good will be followed by something bad because — and despite the concept of grace — well, you just never know.

Destitute The poor people we prayed for who were probably better off than we were, but we didn't know it.

Devil Non-Lutheran word for "Satan."

Dig 1. To tear up something like dirt for a new grave. 2. To think something is really "cool," as in "Wow. I really dig your two-tone saddle shoes."

Dip 1. How the pastor gets water on the baby for baptism. 2. A modern white concoction served with potato chips by town people. 3. A depression in the road by the church. 4. An old-fashioned word for "nerd." 5. What Lutheran farm kids did in the coulee after baling. (Those who liked to make a big deal of things called it "skinny dipping.")

Dish This is a very confusing word for new Lutherans, non-Lutherans, and those visiting the Midwest. 1. A shallow bowl or plate to place food on. 2. A sort of food that is easy to make that you don't mind sharing, as in "Please bring a dish to share." (This would not be an empty dish. It could be a "hotdish.") 3. A Swedish Lutheran blond with nice legs. (This could be a "hot dish," but it could also be kind of an empty one upstairs, if you know what we mean.)

Dixie Cup Because Lutheran Sunday School kids are only treated to these once a year (at the Annual Sunday School Picnic), church fathers decided it wasn't necessary to rename these delicacies (eaten with a small tongue depressor) "Yankee Frozen Dairy Cattle Treats."

Do 1. To perform an act or action, to be in the process of "doing" something like cutting bars or barley. 2. A reference to a woman's hair, as in "Do you like my new do that Veronica gave me?" 3. A Lutheran word for events held at church where either a lot of people came, or there was an awfully long program, such as "Oh mercy me. It was such a big to-do."

Doctrine 1. The teachings that Martin Luther gave us to memorize, learn, and live by. 2. What a sick Scandinavian patient (who isn't really so patient) asks the clinic receptionist, "Doctrine?"

Doeth A Shakespearean word found in the King James Version for people with speech impediments that means to "get on with the program."

Dove 1. A Biblical bird of peace kind of like a barn pigeon, only with better manners. 2. How Donald Sverdup got to the bottom of the lake to get Sharon Ekkedahl's class ring on Skip Day.

Dragon 1. A sea monster in the 'Book of Psalms.' 2. What a bad sermon seems to do.

Drawer 1. One who draws pictures in Sunday School. 2. A wooden bin in the church kitchen for the funeral tablecloths.

Drive 1. An effort to collect outgrown clothes to send overseas. 2. What Lutheran farmers do after their naps on Sunday afternoons so they can check the fields to see who has been cultivating crooked. Like Tollef Amundson said back in '53 when he saw his neighbor's bean field, "Hmm. Looks like he's been trying to spell Sivert Sivertson." 3. Gumption.

Due 1. A sum of money (like a quarter) that Luther Leaguers paid annually. 2. Something tied to a reason or excuse like, "Due to the pastor's sore throat, we will read responsively today." 3. Right

over there, as in "The Arsvold farm is due East."
4. A modern way to say, "And when it was her time to be delivered."

Dust The origin of mankind, and the downfall of Lutheran women.

Duster 1. A feathery thing used to dust the house. 2. A lightweight bathrobe one wears when dusting the house. 3. The person wearing the robe who is dusting the house. 4. A small airplane that sprays the crops.

E...

Earful This is a Lutheran word to describe a particularly lengthy fire and brimstone sermon often based on the Old Testament as in, "Ya, we sure got an earful today. Who was that Jehoshaphat character anyway?"

Earthly Possessions To help ensure a heavenly hereafter, Scandinavian-Lutherans don't want to acquire too many of these. Basically all one needs are a few pails, a potato masher, flashlight and cow, some chickens, rhubarb plants, scatter rugs, a hammer and a pipe organ, a springtooth or drag for the fields, some lye, an apple tree, empty fruit jars, and a '57 Chevy and one is pretty well set.

Easter The one day when town kids picked eggs, and the only time breakfast was served in church. A Lutheran High Holy Day when cars were washed, little girls' new nylon see-through dresses were worn, chin straps on little girls' hats snapped back and bit them, and the relatives came over to have canned, pagan, foreign fruit on top of ham.

Easter Monday A day that causes great consternation for rural Norwegian-American Lutheran women. Should they go ahead and wash clothes or is this a sacred holiday? If they don't do laundry, their whole week will be thrown off and what with the garden to plant and Confirmation doings coming up . . . . What's a woman to do? If it's a secular holiday where work is permitted, why is it hooked on to Easter? And then, after that big ham dinner and all the company, if they don't get the gravy stains outta the good tablecloth, have they wasted frivolous earthly possessions and well, what then?

Ecumenical One of those things that sounds better than it really is, kind of like a "free lunch."

Edgy How Mrs. Arnulf Ellertson, the circle leader, would get when the next Bible study was based on Proverbs 31:10-31.

Education Hour A high church word for "Sunday School."

Education Wing A high church word for "Sunday School Rooms."

Efficient A Lutheran virtue right up there with "accountable" and "clean," especially as practiced and perfected by Lutheran women; applicable to all facets of life, except dusting and washing windows where efficiency didn't pay off. Only elbow grease and hours at the task did.

Egg Coffee Coffee that is boiled in white enamel pots with raw eggs. Just the smell of it drifting up to the sanctuary from the basement of the church is enough to make any good pastor shorten her up a bit and get down to what a funeral is all about — eating and drinking coffee with the neighbors.

Egg Shells 1. What you dropped into the two-gallon enamel coffee pot after stirring the egg and coffee mixture. 2. A sensible, no-cost, nontoxic fertilizer for violets. 3. What church basement women walked on when the pastor's Mrs. showed up for Aid.

Elbow Macaroni An Italian pasta made Lutheran by boiling it too much and creaming it to death, and made nutritious and wholesome by adding sliced, leftover wieners.

Electric Hammond Organ A tinny sounding piece of furniture bought with memorials to replace that big, overbearing, 50-year-old, magnificent-sounding instrument that would wake over-the-hill farmers from a dead sleep when all the stops were pulled. *Soli deo gloria.*

Emotional Outbursts A plague that some Lutheran girls with hormonal imbalance were prone to at donkey basketball games.

Enamelware Chipped, cheap, church pots and kettles that held egg coffee and *lutefisk* and matched the church dishes if they were white, and the Concordia Hymnal if they were blue.

Endow 1. High church word for "memorials." 2. Vague reference to bosom of the broader variety. (See also **Bosom**.)

Engagement This does not mean "meeting" or "appointment" in Lutheran language. It means that Sylvia has promised to marry Darrell and settle down on the homeplace.

Equal Amounts This was another Lutheran virtue practiced wherever food was served irrespective of the size, age, or gender of the recipient of the food.

Eve 1. The time of day when Lutherans had Vesper Services and sang 'Now The Day Is Over.' 2. The woman in the Bible ultimately responsible for dust, snakes, and good girdles. (See **Dust** and **Good Girdle**.)

Excelsis A word we sing at Christmas that is

probably Latin for "egg shells."

Eyeballing It Up 1. The ability to line up the church basement's eight-foot long banquet tables in a straight row by only using the pattern in the linoleum floor as a guide. 2. The knack of cutting pan after pan of Lutheran bars into uniform sizes to exactly match the crowd in attendance, and still be able to send a few extra home with the bachelor farmers.

F...

F. Melius The real father of four-part Lutheran harmony who was probably easier to get to know on a first name basis than Martin Luther. People who sang under F. Melius — or wished they had — never referred to him as "Dr. Christiansen." Same thing with his son, the next father of Lutheran music, who was best known as "Paul J." We always called Martin Luther, "Luther" and never just "Martin."

Face Cards Colorful abstract drawings that represent the devil, the mayor of Las Vegas and his Mrs., and a shovel designed to dig one's way straight down to hell.

Fading A word that is often accompanied by "wilting" to describe either a lack of color, as in "Oh, those funeral flowers are fading and wilting so fast they almost look dead," or a lack of stamina, as in "Ya, you know, Arnold's Mrs., well she's just fading away so fast now. Sure thought she'd make it through Christmas!"

Fair-Weather This phrase is used three ways among Lutherans. 1. "It's so sunny and such fair weather." 2. "It's such good Fair weather, let's load up the kids, go see the 4-H barns and demolition derby, and eat at the Lutheran lunch stand." 3. "She's some sort of fair-weather friend. Yesterday she said the Black Hymnal was good enough for her, and today at the Annual Meeting she went and voted for the new Red."

Faithful Unto the End Someone who didn't miss church even when sick, who served when called, who didn't falter or waiver when temptations arose, who didn't fall short and go dancing, and one who bequeathed a large sum of money to the church.

Familiar Hymns This phrase is generally preceded by "good old," and forms the basis for sound congregational life unto the children of the third and fourth generations. Newcomer Lutheran composers like John Ylvisaker and Ray McKeever fight this concept.

Farewell Sermon In importance — but not content — this rates right up there with the Sermon on the Mount. It is a pastor's farewell and final warning to his flock before he moves on to greener pastures. He spent a lot of time on it so he'd be invited back to the Centennial.

Fast and Loose This is a Lutheran plague referring to town women who didn't work or own property, and to young girls who wear pink lipstick and
training bras and skip junior choir practice. It is a
favorite warning from Lutheran mothers, i.e.,
"Don't go near the bulls when you get to the County
Fair and also stay away from those fast and loose
women in short-shorts."

Fatherland (See **Holy Land**.)

Featured Speaker Someone from out of the
county who drives a newer model car and has a
high opinion of himself.

Feelings This word was only in Luther's <u>Original</u>
Small Dictionary and refers to his passion for Kitty,
My Rib. It has been left out of the Scandinavian-
American translation because feelings don't exist
among Scandinavian-American Lutherans and, if
they did, one wouldn't talk about it so the word
isn't necessary. If you hear the phrase, "Elmer,
please share your feelings with us," you can pretty
well bet the farm that you took a wrong turn and
ended up in a Unitarian Church.

Fellowship This was traditionally a noun that
meant a serious, no-nonsense get together. With

the advent of the Green Hymnal, this became a verb, as in "Make plans to worship and fellowship with us." Featured Speakers would use this word. (See **Featured Speaker**.)

Fellowship Buffet A high church word for "pot-luck."

Fence-Sitter A word used in two circumstances in the Lutheran Church. 1. To describe someone who can't make up his mind about keeping the Black or buying the new Red Hymnal. 2. One, who if he has an opinion about sending Luther League delegates to the national convention, won't express it out loud.

Fend for Yourself 1. The prime Scandinavian-American Lutheran virtue from which all others stem. (See also **Accept, Clean, Order**, etc.) 2. A concept that kicks in at two months of age and continues throughout life.

Fermented Grape Juice A controversial subject brought on by the lack of knowledge of Latin and a lack of experience with wine.

Fester A word to describe the action of body boils prevalent among FFA boys, and of mental ones prevalent among old men after the Annual Meeting.

Festival An activity — usually secular and occurring in town in the summer — that borders on sin but is sanctioned by the rural Lutheran powers-that-be when a visiting missionary is in the area right after a good crop. Thus, there are Mission or Harvest Festivals where Lutherans can share the bounty and blessings with the less fortunate, and drink some egg coffee.

Fidget What little Lutherans do when the sermon is too long, and what older Lutherans do when it hits too close to home.

Fig Leaf An Early Christian jockstrap more for cover-up than comfort or protection.

Filmstrip Silent movies sent by Augsburg Publishing House to augment Sunday School lessons about the mission fields. These were never used by real missionaries. Real missionaries had slides and did less censoring.

Final Resting Place A misnomer for "cemetery" because real Lutherans know this isn't really final.

Finger Plays Show and Tell programs that pre-school Lutherans perform at the Annual Christmas Program. This doesn't require memorization, and often the fingers found their way up a nose; never in rehearsal, only in performance.

Finger Sandwiches Fancy town sandwiches smeared with deadspreads, stacked and glued together, and occasionally served at Lutheran wedding receptions in the church basement if the bride was the minister's daughter or if aunts were coming from Ames or Rapid City. (See **Dead-spreads**.)

Finish Everything on Your Plate An informal Lutheran commandment that wasn't given a number or ever asked at Public Questioning, but goes a long way towards explaining why 22W is the most common dress size in the Lutheran Church Basement kitchen.

Finnish 1. Another brand of Lutheranism that had some direct "apostolic" connection. 2. A kind of Lutheran who grew great strawberries and was cleaner than average.

Fire and Brimstone A Black Hymnal term that meant "behave, act decent, don't get your name in the newspaper, and turn out or you're asking for eternal trouble."

First-Born Although many Lutherans left the Old Country because of primogeniture, the first born was also put to work in the New Country. Probably because Lutheran families were so small, and one never knew if there'd be more helpers, these first-born babies were worked hard, i.e., the draft horse of the family.

Fish A Catholic food that Scandinavian-American Lutherans were only obligated to eat once a year at the Annual *Lutefisk* Supper, and German Lutherans were never required to eat.

Fish Pond A secular activity from the school carnival that made its way into the church basement for the Harvest Festival. Normal prizes included dish rags, nickel tablets, apples, hankies, pencils, crocheted crosses, and leftover Cracker Jack prizes.

Fishy Smell 1. How the church still smells 18 weeks after the Annual *Lutefisk* Supper. 2. When "something's rotten in Denmark" and there's more brewing in the church than the egg coffee.

Fixture in the Church 1. Gold, ivory, and pale-colored hanging glass lights that replaced kerosene lanterns at Lutheran Churches. 2. Widow Kleppevik, the last living Charter Member. (See **Charter Member**.)

Flamboyant This is not a Lutheran word.

Flame 1. A light that Lutherans hoped would be kept small, such as the Advent candles and the pilot light in the church kitchen. 2. A new beau that Cheryl's mom hoped would be <u>the</u> one, as in "Ya, you know, she's got a new flame. That Snesrud guy from over Elbow Lake way."

Flashy Dresser This is not a Lutheran word either.

Flat as a Pancake A phrase that isn't a compliment among Lutherans even when it is used in reference to a pancake. Also used in reference to bosoms, altos, and to sermons that lack fire and "meat." (See also **Alto**, **Bosom**, and **Meat**.)

Fleece 1. A nice noun for "sheep wool." 2. A bad verb for "swindle."

Flesh 1. Something religious that dwelt among us. 2. The fatty part of women and of different cuts of meat. 3. A word used to describe our skin in a carnal state, sort of a necessary evil.

Flood 1. (See **Noah**.) 2. A "dig" at a Lutheran boy who grew faster than his mom could let down the hem of his pants legs, as in "Hey, Hick! Waitin' for a flood?"

Floors 1. In Lutheranism, what must be cleaned in the same way we are taught to pray, i.e., without ceasing! 2. The levels of a house, as in "The bed-

rooms are on the second floor." (Churches didn't
have different floors. Instead, Lutheran Churches
had the basement, the main church, and the
steeple.)

Flour Sack The container for the most Lutheran
staple of all, flour. These containers were washed
up and used to sew little girls' dresses and for
sewing aprons to sell at the bazaar.

Flowers Before the Red Hymnal these provided
the only color in the sanctuary. They were grown
and placed on the altar for normal Sundays by
Bothilda Torkelson for 43 years. They were also
needed in bouquets for weddings and funerals, in
corsages for Mother's Day, "boutonniere" style for
ushers and Confirmands, and for centerpieces at
Silvers. Seasonal Lutheran varieties included
Easter lilies, carnations, lilacs, peonies, zinnias,
and glads. (See **Boutonniere** and **Silvers**.)

Flunk What would have happened to the Christof-
ferson boy at Catechization if the minister had
asked the wrong question. (See also **Piece of
Cake**.)

Flush 1. A kind of toilet installed in town
churches in the 30s, and in country churches in the
50s. 2. How Mrs. Arnulf Bergquist wanted to look
in her new Easter hat and coat. 3. What happened

to Jerome's face when Inga Julseth winked at him.

Flustered This describes the Sunday School superintendent's demeanor from Thanksgiving through the Annual Christmas Program.

Fly Paper A sticky, but humane, Lutheran device invented to make summer meals more pleasant. It looked like a shotgun shell before it was opened, and like vertical yellow crepe paper after it was opened.

Fly Poison When Fly Paper just won't cut it, make Lutheran Fly Poison by mixing one table-spoon of formaldehyde and 14 cups of sugar in half a pint of rainwater. Set in saucers in sunny win-dows. It's not dangerous to Lutherans unless they drink it.

Foam Rubber The only kind of dice that Luther-ans hoods had. Not to be played with, just admired.

Folding Table How Lutherans pronounce "card table" when they are in church.

Food Something Lutherans need to have every time they go to church.

Footing What Gunnar Huseth poured to hold the new church up, and what he lost on the sidewalk to pull him down.

For Better or Worse A Lutheran wedding phrase that is easy to say, but tough to carry out.

Foreign Brazil, France, Italy, Ireland, Mexico, Spain, and any other Catholic strongholds.

Foretaste Something Lutherans say in the liturgy but don't understand nearly as clearly as "after-taste." (See *Lutefisk*.)

Fortress 1. Usually proceeded by "A Mighty." 2. A contemporary way of saying Augsburg Publishing House. 3. A place by Abercrombie, ND.

Foundation 1. What the church was built on. (See **Footing**.) 2. What high school girls who were going steady put on under their rouge. 3. A garment usually called a good girdle. (See **Corset**.)

Four-Bucklers What Bernard Thorson's five-bucklers became when he slipped and tore both the top buckles off as he climbed over the barbed-wire fence to release a stuck pheasant.

Four-Part The ultimate in Lutheran harmony.

Free Thinker Those who challenged the status quo of Lutherans, taught at Lutheran colleges, dodged the draft, kept their maiden names when they married, and changed the gender of words in the Green Hymnal without batting an eyelash or experiencing any Lutheran guilt.

Free Will Offering A misnomer because it was never "free," and Lutherans weren't usually that willing.

Freer A noun, not an adjective. Lutherans who took off on their own when the Red Hymnal came out, and now send their offspring to a Bible school in Medicine Lake, MN. (See **High Church/Low Church**.)

French Seam A foreign sewing stitch that Lutheran women used on their Christmas dresses if they planned to enter it in the "Make It With Wool" Contest at the County Fair.

Fresh 1. Rhubarb. 2. Town boys.

Frizzy The result from keeping Richard Hudnut on too long. (See **Perm**.)

Front End Where the crank was on the Model T, and where he was in the sanctuary.

Frugal Another Lutheran virtue that began in the Old Country and was given a booster shot during

The Depression.

Fruitcake 1. A cake made with foreign-sounding fruit that you give and receive, and it's never the first to go. It is a good present for the Sunday School teacher because it lasts at least until Easter. It also makes a good paperweight and doorstop. 2. A pillar of the Lutheran Church who has lost her marbles. (See **Pillar**.)

Full 1. What Norwegian Lutherans got who ate too much *rømmegrøt*. 2. What German Lutherans got who drank too much dark beer.

Full-Figured A nice and politically-correct way to describe a fat Lutheran woman.

Fuming Mad How Willie Bolstad felt after the Annual Meeting where the majority voted to pad the pews.

Fun and Games Among Lutherans this phrase is used infrequently.

Fundraisers These come in various forms at various times because Lutherans aren't the greatest at tithing. (See also **Accountable, Car Wash, Collection, Frugal, Harvest Festival,** *Lutefisk* **Supper, Mission Festival,** etc.)

Funeral Director A dead-end job.

Funeral Fan Not a person who goes from funeral to funeral to get autographs, but a handheld cardboard thing on a handle given to mourners by the undertaker.

Funeral Shoes Worn by the living (who served in the kitchen.)

Funeral Suit Worn by the dead (and purchased for the youngest child's wedding.)

Funny Paper What some parents read when their kids are at Sunday School.

Furlough What missionaries and servicemen go on. Pastors go "on leave." Usually this means they have packed up the whole family and headed to a Bible Camp where the pastor will spend his one-week "leave" leading junior high campers in Bible Study, and picking up a few extra bucks while having quality time with the family. (See **Buck**.)

Fuses 1. Something that always blew during the Annual *Lutefisk* Supper. 2. Something that was always short on German Lutheran men.

Fyda An acceptable bad word because no one knows what it means.

Gadabout A busybody who sits in the bakery drinking coffee and talking to people she hardly knows, while her work at home goes undone.

Gall Something Lutherans sing about in connection with wormwood, and something older people have removed related to the bladder. (See **Wormwood and the Gall.**)

Games in the Basement Shuffleboard and Wink 'em.

Garterbelt A restrictive device designed to hold up a little girl's long brown or white stockings, and to destroy her attention span.

Garters 1. Devices designed to hold up men's dress socks and only worn to church. 2. The kind of snake that crawls around in cemeteries.

Gas-Guzzlers Cars that required ethyl because of their big 318 cubic inch engines and big tail fins, which were driven by show-offs, people from Texas, and hoods who wanted to make a statement.

Gathered Circle Skirt The second Home Ec sewing project. (The first was a cobbler apron; the third was a tank top.) These had side zippers and, along with wearing them to the school's Spring Style Show, Lutheran girls were expected to wear them to church for a few years until they outgrew them.

Gaudy Red dangly earrings, the Red Hymnal, red aisle carpets, red pew cushions, and the Advent wreath.

Gaunt A caved-in, pale, physical condition rarely seen in the Lutheran Church kitchen until someone was on her last leg.

Gay A word to describe a pretty print dress with rickrack on the sleeves.

Gel 1. A contemporary name for waveset. 2. What chokecherries and strawberries could do under the right condition. 3. What *lutefisk* did under the wrong condition. 4. What the ideas in Harvey Lundstrom's mind couldn't do under any condition.

Gelatin A tasteless, orderless form of Jell-O that fancy town women took in tablet form because they read in movie magazines that it would help them grow fancy fingernails. (Women from the farm had no need for long fingernails because they just got in the way, took to long to clean, and weren't very Christian.)

General Delivery How — until the inventions of zip codes and C-Sections — most mail and most Lutheran babies were brought forth.

Genes We're not real sure. No one ever went into detail on this.

Germs Something that lurks all over but can't be seen, heard, smelled, nor felt, but it can kill Lutherans. A plague that originated in the Garden of Eden along with snakes and dust.

Ghost 1. A Black and Red Hymnal word that the Green Hymnal, politically-correct folks changed to "spirit." 2. To describe the lack of color, as in the color Nellie Nelson turned when she found Nels slumped over his "Termos" against the back wheel of the Allis — but he was only taking a snooze, i.e., "She turned white as a ghost."

Gideons Men who didn't belong to your congregation but showed up once a year and got you to put a buck on their open Bible at the back of the church after services so heathens in hotels would have something to read when the T.V. was all snowy. (See **Buck**.)

Gift of Gab What Tillie Swenson was blessed with.

Giggle What junior high girls did in church every time they saw a Lutheran boy.

Gingersnap Pronounced "yin-yer snap," this is the best dunkin' cookie of all.

Girth (See **Finish Everything On Your Plate**.)

Glad/Glads 1. How your heart should be. 2. The kind of flowers furnished by Bothilda Torkelson for Gus Guttormson's funeral.

Glitter and Glue Except for pictures of heathen women, this was the only thing that put some flair into Sunday School.

Glob The quantity of butter that Gunnar Tingvold put on his *lefse*, mashed potatoes, *lutefisk*, *flatbrød*, peas, and lap at the Annual *Lutefisk* Supper.

Gloria Dei Agnes's sister who lived four miles south of town, wore lipstick, played cards, went steady, and overcame these shortcomings and made it into the hymnal on every fifth page. (See *Agnus Dei*.)

Gloves These were the mainstay of the Lutheran uniform in the Black Hymnal era and were accompanied by hats for both men and women. Now cloth ones are used only by handbell ringers in the Lutheran Church, and plastic ones are used by finicky kitchen workers who grew up in town and have allergies.

Gnash Something we don't want to spend eternity doing with our teeth. Pronounced "Nash," but a Nash is a car for poor Lutherans.

Godmother A Catholic's female sponsor.

Golden 1. Unlike Silvers, this anniversary was commonly called "their 50th," not "their Golden." But — like Silvers — the bride had to doll herself up and wear her good girdle, and the groom looked just as uncomfortable as he had at their Silver. The program at the 50th was shorter than it had been at the 25th, because everyone wanted to get home before dark even though most of the couple's friends had sold off their cattle and moved to town or were gone. 2. A rule that we try to live by. 3. The color of a calf in the Old Testament when beef prices were higher.

Good Girdle The ultimate torture device that Lutheran women wore brought on by Eve's doings in the Garden of Eden, right up there above snakes, dust, and germs. (See **Foundation**.)

Good Gravy 1. A compliment to the cook. 2. Appropriate Lutheran slang for, "*Uffda*, what next!"

Good Grooming What Lutheran 4-H'rs specialize in up to, and during, Fair Week.

Good Reading Material Tracts and pamphlets put out by Augsburg Publishing house or Zondervan, Ideal magazine, poems by Helen Steiner Rice, *Julhefte*, and the Ola and Per comic strip in the *Decorah Posten*. (See also **Reading Material**.)

Goose Bumps Town word for "goose pimples."

Gooseberry This has nothing to do with geese, but is a kind of dessert sauce that gives Lutherans their only opportunity to pucker in public.

Gossip A way to catch up on the latest without subscribing to the local paper and it is cheaper, generally more accurate, and doesn't turn one's fingers black. It proliferates in the church basement. (See **Backfire**.)

Grace 1. Undeserved goodness. 2. How Pearl Nygaard acted under pressure, like when she was in charge of the lunch for the pastor's mother's funeral and the current went out. 3. A little note that accompanists hated, but was found in most sheet music. 4. The younger sister of Agnes and Gloria Day who some people called "Amazing," and who also turned out. (See *Agnus Dei*, *Gloria Dei*, and **Current**.)

Grape Juice What Trefoldighet Lutheran used for communion because no one would drive to Watertown to buy the Mogen David.

Graveyard Low church word for "cemetery."

Greased Watermelon Contest The best game at Luther Crest Bible Camp.

Green Beans The stuff that floats in Cream of Mushroom soup and is covered with canned French-fried onion rings and is served at potlucks in the town church.

Greetings A salutation of great joy brought by the angels, and what someone at church brings from someone at synod headquarters who didn't feel like driving on country roads. (See **Behalf**.)

Grip 1. A suitcase used for Bible Camp and

Luther League conventions. 2. The blacksmith, Virgil Tollefson's, handshake. (See also **Host**.)

Groom 1. A noun for the star male attraction at a wedding. 2. A verb for what Lutheran 4-H kids do to themselves and their heifers.

Grounds 1. The property around the church that must be spruced up for the Centennial. 2. Crunchy residue in the bottom of the egg coffee pot that you throw by a tree for angle worms so you can go fishing. 3. A reason for divorce or other tough action, as in "Ya, well, on what grounds?"

Guilt This, along with a fear that your child will "turn," are the two things that Catholics and Lutherans have in common.

H...

Habakkuk A seventh-century prophet with a non-Lutheran name.

Habit Something that Catholic nuns wear and other people have.

Hail Mary A kind of football pass that Lutherans don't throw.

Hairnet A respectable alternative to a hat (especially if it was beaded) used to protect a Lutheran woman's crowning glory and to keep her perm intact and some loose hairs out of the *lutefisk*; a few steps below a halo. (See **Frizzy**, **Halo**, and **Perm**.)

Half-and-Half A poor substitute for separated cream. It is used mainly by town women who are watching their figures and don't give two hoots about keeping their strength up.

Half-breed The offspring of a mixed marriage, such as one with a Norwegian Lutheran father and a Swedish Lutheran mother.

Half-Hearted How the young seminarian's wife, who had grown up in Hopkins, felt about her life-long helpmeet's call to Cresco, IA. (See **Lifelong Helpmeet**.)

Hall What we would deck with holly if we belonged to another religious group, and where we would be sent if we decked another kid.

Hallelujah What Scandinavian Lutherans proclaim out loud once a year, which is about as often as they can handle such an outburst in public.

Halo 1. A pretty wreath that floats above the angels' heads that we all want to have someday. 2. How Mrs. Jesper Bugge answers the telephone.

Hamper 1. A verb for what the pastor's wife did to the Sunday School superintendent's progress with the preschool when she intervened. 2. The most common Lutheran wedding gift in the 50s.

Hand-Me-Downs Something that starts out growing in a field or on an animal and goes through various stages and numerous generations and finally ends up either on the Mission Field or in a scatter rug.

Handbells Glittery instruments that took over when steeples became outdated. (See also **Gloves**.)

Handbook A pamphlet sent to future students upon acceptance at a Lutheran college designed to scare them, but to comfort their parents, which contains the do's and don'ts of dorm life like stuff about the doors locking at 10:00 p.m., meal tickets, dress codes for Sunday, the legality of popcorn poppers, chapel attendance, the opposite sex, floor devotions, train schedules, and phone numbers to call if one is troubled, i.e., the campus pastor or the campus shrink.

Handkerchief 1. What Lutherans blew their noses on in public when their sleeves just wouldn't do, and what Catholics wore on their heads when they forgot a hat. 2. A piece of cloth, which when knotted in the corner, became a mock coin purse for poor rural Sunday School kids' nickels.

Handle 1. What kept falling off Bruflat Lutheran's oven door. 2. What Harvey Lundstrom couldn't seem to be able to do with things very well. (See **Gel**.)

Hang Up 1. What the men did with their storm-coats in the vestibule, and what Minnie Ulsager did

when the Stewardship Chairman telephoned her.
2. A kind of phobia exhibited by shy people.

Hanger A free wire contraption that could be transformed into a padded, crocheted, scented "garment holder" for the bazaar costing $3.50; a semi-pliable metal frame that could be bent to form the Christmas angel's halo. (See **Halo**.)

Hangman A quiet game that Lutheran kids play on the church bulletin that seems a little more worldly than Tic Tac Toe.

Hans Nielsen Hauge Sort of a cross between Jesse Helms and Jesse Ventura who knew what he stood for and made no bones about it, later becoming the leader of the Haugean movement among Norwegian-American Lutherans. (See **Revival** and **Piety**.)

Hard What memorization, Catechization, and farming was.

Hard-Boiled 1. A kind of egg that allowed Lutheran Church Basement Women to say the word "devil" right out loud in church. 2. How Old Man Larson got after his wife left him.

Hard-Core An inflexible Norwegian Lutheran.

Hard-Headed An inflexible German Lutheran.

Hard-Nosed An inflexible Swedish Lutheran.

Hardtop 1. The surface of the parking lot at the Lutheran Church in town. 2. A kind of convertible that the hymnal salesman drove. It wasn't much of a convertible at all. (See **Oxymoron**.)

Harmony (See **F. Melius** and **Four-Part**.)

Haute Cuisine French for *lutefisk*.

Haven What the haybarn was for the kids, and the outhouse was for the men.

Hayride A Lutheran-sanctioned, well-chaperoned mode of transportation for a first date.

Head Cheese A Lutheran immigrant cheese made by boiling up parts of dead animal heads, and that's just the way it looked and tasted.

Headquarters A place where people who liked to call the shots hung out.

Heathens People without names who didn't wear much clothes and who lived overseas and appeared in filmstrips — kind of likc foreign movie stars.

Heavy-Duty Something that is strongly constructed for the long haul like the church bell and German Lutherans. (See also **Spic-and-Span**, **Stormcoat**, and **Thermal Underwear**.)

Heel 1. The skinny part of a woman's shoe that got stuck in the furnace grate when she went up for altar offering at Thanksgiving. 2. A nickname for Ricky Chiseler.

Hefty Synonymous with Lutheran Church Basement Women.

Hell A word Lutherans rarely said but when they did, they pronounced it "H — E — Double Toothpicks."

Helpmeet A Biblical word for "spouse." (See **Lifelong Helpmeet** and **Plain Jane**.)

Herald 1. The name of Concordia Lutheran Church's newsletter. 2. The first name of the hired hand at Aasen's farm. 3. The angel's p.a. system.

Heresy An opinion contrary to common belief. In the Lutheran Church this could involve anything from Red Hymnals to drums to carpet to ashes on the forehead to dancing to pierced ears to Cool Whip to slip-on shoes to dial telephones to one-part music to coed dorms to horseless carriages, etc.

Hide 1. To protect and conceal. 2. The outer layer of an animal stripped off. (This got very confusing to immigrants with broken English when the Hymn of the Day was 'Hide Me, O My Savior Hide!'

High Church/Low Church The crux of the matter. (See **Freer**, **Hans Nielsen Hauge**, and **Headquarters**.)

Hindsight 1. A view of the back of the minister. 2. Twenty-twenty vision.

Hip Fractures One of the three legitimate excuses for "not serving." (See **Blood Clots** and **Death**.)

Hitch A good Lutheran word to know because it has so many uses. 1. How you hook the trailer to the Studebaker to bring the bales to the church for the manger. 2. A kind of post old Lutherans tied their horses to during services. 3. How the Maloney kid got a ride to the State Fair. 4. What Oscar Lang did to his pants, i.e., "He hitched 'em up." 5. An obstacle to prevent something from happening, like Gunnar Gubberud's shyness. (See **Housekeeper**.) 6. What Gunnar and Klara should have done from the start, i.e., "got hitched."

Hokey-Pokey A form of "square gaming," kind of like the Bunny Hop, that was almost a dance and was permitted under certain circumstances. (Non-Lutheran food for thought: What if the Hokey-Pokey really is what it's all about???) (See also **Alumni**.)

Holden Village A place out West where Christians who weren't farmers could go to experience nature, help with dishes, "fellowship," and read Jonathan Livingston's 'Seagull.' (See **Fellowship**, **Good Reading Material** and **Reading Material**.)

Holding Hands This does not refer to the pagan practice of playing cards, but it is still borderline behavior for Lutheran kids. (See also **Buddy System**.)

Holidays Christmas, Easter, and Thanksgiving; *lutefisk*, ham, and turkey.

Hollyhocks Farm flowers that little Lutherans made dolls out of that grew well along fences, sheds, and outhouses, but didn't stand so well in a vase.

Hollywood The ultimate sin city where sexpots strutted, people did their nails, and women smoked cigarettes, all in the name of vanity.

Holy City Jerusalem, or Decorah, IA.

Holy Land Nazareth, Norway, Sweden, Denmark, Iceland, Finland, and Germany. (See **Fatherland**.)

Holy Roman Empire A place overseas that German Lutherans are acquainted with where monks ate *brats* and drank dark beer, and where the Lutheran tradition of splitting and merging began. (See **Merging and Splitting**.)

Home Visits A scary time when the pastor came for coffee and Mom put on a clean apron, Dad hosed down the manure scraper by the door, and the kids volunteered to do the barn chores.

Homebound What shut-ins, who are "wisited" by the Sunshine Club, are.

Honeymoon The one time when farmers could leave for two or three days to go to the North Shore or Itasca State Park if they were from Minnesota; the Peace Gardens if they were from North Dakota, Manitoba or Saskatchewan; the Dells if they were from Wisconsin; the Corn Palace if they were from South Dakota; and the Nordic Fest if they were from Iowa.

Hoods 1. The front ends of pickups and cars most prone to hail damage. 2. The part of a sweatshirt that should cover the head but has lost its cord, and the part of the outfit that friars wear so no one can see that they're Catholic. 3. The Maloney brothers just down the road a piece.

Hoops 1. What the Ladies Guild uses to embroider handiwork for the bazaar. 2. What the Ladies Guild jumps through to get new pickle dishes. 3. A kind of undergarment the immigrants wore to make their waists look tiny. (See **Petticoat** and **Cancan**.)

Hope Chest 1. A modern version of an immigrant trunk in which young Lutheran girls placed embroidered dishtowels and starched doilies they had received from their aunts for their birthdays with the hope that these would be put to use before they, the young Lutheran girls, ended up in the Old Age Home. 2. A training bra.

Horns 1. The pointed protrusions on the heads of the devil, steers, and Vikings. 2. What the boys' brass ensemble played on Easter Sunday, i.e., one French horn, one tuba, and nine cornets. (See also **Shoe Horn**.)

Hospital The "Alpha and Omega" for many Lutherans, and an appropriate place for Lutheran women to work when they quit farming and moved to town. (See **Alpha and Omega**.)

Hospital Corners The Bible Camp way to make a

84

bed.

Host 1. The uncle of the bride with a good grip who welcomes guests to the reception in the church basement and points to the punch bowl. 2. A name given to the white cardboard-tasting circle that is served at communion when no one has time to bake bread. 3. *'Den Store Hvite Flok.'*

Hot Water Something you want to soak in before church, but don't want to <u>get</u> in at church.

Hotdish 1. Low church word for "casserole;" a rib-sticking, often pale, high cholesterol delivery system for leftovers and soup that has sustained Lutherans since they came over on the boat. 2. Not to be confused with a "hot dish" which is a blond bombshell wearing a strapless gown and falsies at the junior-senior banquet.

Hotflash An abrupt increase in both temperature and temper that leaves a woman looking like a limp dishrag, and feeling like the key on a can of Spam that's gone off track, i.e., she can't go forward, she can't go backward, she just dangles and is good for nothing. (See **Spam**.)

Housedress Not really a dress <u>for</u> a house, but an easily washable dress worn <u>in</u> the house when a woman is dressing <u>up</u> the house, painting, dusting, mopping, canning, etc.

Houseflies Pesky little seasonal things that like the smell and taste of Lutheran cooking more than most Lutherans do. (See **Fly Poison**.)

Housekeeper What they called women who lived in sin with bachelors, like Klara Klubberud who moved in with Gunnar Gubberud who was too shy to propose.

How Is This Done? One of life's most perplexing questions introduced into 'Luther's Small Catechism' by Martin himself, repeated frequently by Confirmation students who were busy memorizing, and applied thereafter into all aspects of Christian and secular life by confirmed Lutherans. For example, "The body of Christ is in the host." ('How Is This Done?'); "The jars will seal." ('How Is This Done?'); etc. A companion phrase to 'What Does This Mean?' and 'This Is Most Certainly True!'

Husfloen, Richard A professor who got impressionable college freshmen to question more than 'How Is This Done?,' but not too much more.

Hymnals The source of much strife in the Scandinavian Lutheran churches. What was supposed to promote and foster harmony created much disharmony and more new synods.

Hymnal Committee 1. People elected on a synod-wide basis to get small congregations to spend money foolishly. 2. The reason for so many words in this dictionary. (See also **Dedicate**, **Enamelware**, **Fair Weather**, **Familiar Hymns**, **Fellowship**, **Fence-Sitter**, **Fire and Brimstone**, **Flowers**, **Free Thinker**, **Freer**, **Gaudy**, **Ghost**, **Gloves**, **Hardtop**, **Heresy**, **Hymnals**, **Victory**, **Viewpoint**, **Vigil**, **Vigilantes**, etc.)

I...

Iceberg Lettuce There were never green salads in the Lutheran Church before the Green Hymnal came in. Lettuce was used to park the square-cut, orange-carrot Jell-O pieces on at the Mother-Daughter Banquet.

Ice-Cold How Cora Knutson's feet felt when she went into the locker plant to get a roast and she was wearing open-toe shoes, and how cold it really was in '52 when the powers-that-be at Our Savior's Lutheran considered postponing the Annual *Lutefisk* Supper. This is ten degrees colder than "beastly *kaldt*," it doesn't get much colder than that! (See **Beastly *Kaldt*.**)

Ice Cream Containers In a good year, these were Dixie Cups accompanied by little tongue depressors given out at the Annual Sunday School Picnic. In a normal year, these were cardboard, five-gallon things stored in olive green, padded cases (three per case) that looked like something military and were carried by the men who also did the scooping. The five-gallon containers showed up several months later at a bazaar camouflaged as decorative wastebaskets, and pulled in money for the overseas missions.

Ice Cube This is a foreign word not used in Lutheran Churches. These were never found in Lutheran Church Basements, and usually not in Lutheran homes.

Icelander Direct descendants of the Vikings who read sagas and lived by Cavalier, ND, Minneota, MN, or on Washington Island, WI, and had to choose which synod to go to: the Norwegian Lutheran, the Swedish Lutheran, the Danish Lutheran, the Finnish (Apostolic) Lutheran, or the German Lutheran.

Icon Something found in Catholic Churches, and on Lutheran computers.

Icy Roads (See **Slipping**, definition #3.)

Identify What red fingernail-polished initials on cakepans helped women do when the dishes had been washed after a big doings at church.

Idle Another Lutheran plague when applied to

people, as in "Idle hands are the tools of the devil," but it's okay for cars; "Just let her idle when you run in with it."

Idol Just as bad as "idle." As Martin Luther himself explained, "money, property, pleasures and person," and one could add Marilyn Monroe and Elvis Presley. (See **Golden**.)

I'll Dry One of the cheeriest phrases uttered in the church basement kitchen. (For further information, see page 145 in the book, 'Growing Up Lutheran.')

Ill Someone who was poorly and probably doctoring. If someone "took ill," it was time to call the midwife because a delivery was imminent.

Ill-Bred (See **Half-Breed**.)

Ill-Mannered What 4-H kids were put on earth to counteract.

Illegal (See **Dancing**.)

Illegitimate (See **Dancing**.)

Image 1. Something that Luther thought was "graven." 2. What you see back from the cracked mirror on the back of the church kitchen door so you know what you'll look like when you are older.

Immaculate Conception A Catholic phrase that was never used among Lutherans but applied to them as well because in the 30s, 40s, and 50s, no Lutheran woman was ever pregnant. (A few town women "got p.g." in the 50s.) (See also **Ill**.)

Immoral   (See **Dancing**.)

Impaired A word that follows "slightly" and refers mostly to someone's eyesight and the probable need for new spectacles.

Impress This is a bad word that is not practiced by confirmed Lutherans. (See **Worthy**.)

Impure Thoughts Not fully explained so we don't know for sure when we're having them.

In Memory Of . . .   Especially used for the ongoing purchases of new hymnals. (See also **Radio Ministry**, **Stained Glass Windows**, and *Vesterheim*.)

Inadequate This has to do with the church kitchen from the women's point of view, the furnace in the parsonage from the pastor's point of view, and the budget from the pastor's wife's point of view.

Income A rarely used word although Lutherans

know what it means; it means "take in," as in "Ya, how much did we take in, then?"

Indecent This is a vague area like "Impure Thoughts;" not fully explained so not sure when it's happening.

Independence Day 1. In many places, July 4 was the one day like a Sunday that Lutheran farmers took off and joined the town people. In other places, they went out to the cornfields to make sure it was knee-high. 2. A day when ethnic Lutherans could kick up their heels a little bit if all their work was done: Norwegians, May 17; Finns, December 6; Canadians, July 1; Swedes, June 6; Danes, June 5; Icelanders, June 17; Germans, Who knows??!

Index 1. A kind of card for Lutheran recipes to be written on and filed. 2. The finger used most often by mothers when their kids are acting up and behaving like heathens. 3. An alphabetized list of "First Lines of Hymns" found at the back of hymn-books.

Indigestion What Helga Barsness, the Luther League chaperone, got from pizza pie and riding the "Tilt-a-Whirl" at the County Fair.

Industrial Strength A certain kind of *lefse* made from Early Ohio spuds by Mrs. Holger Holverson that was tough, durable, and heavy-duty and could be used for knee-pads when washing the church basement floor and gardening, for shoulder pads in a pinch, and for emergency shingles when the steeple blew down.

Ingredients Stuff you put into something, like cookies and marriages, that is directly proportional to the outcome.

Iniquity Something bad that will happen to our children down to the third and fourth generations if we blow it now.

Injure 1. A bloody cut from falling off a bike. 2. Something related to the Fifth Commandment and to the "least of them."

Insane A modern word for "nuts."

Instinct How Lutheran women could tell how much food to prepare, and how Lutheran men knew how much seed to get.

Institute 1. Something that has to do with the Passover and the Sacrament of the Altar, i.e., communion. 2. A place where one can learn more, like at Lutheran Bible Institute (LBI).

Insulation What it takes to get through a Midwestern winter, i.e., haybales, long Johns, tar paper, lard, etc. (See **Lard, Stormcoat** and **Thermal Underwear**.)

Insurance AAL and LB. Even Lutherans with a great deal of faith have to consider this.

Intercede/Intercession Lutherans don't have to go through Mary or the saints, but can dial heaven directly. (Sometimes, though, we need the pastor to help find the number.)

Interdenominational Cooperation An old-fashioned word for "ecumenism" used to describe the phenomenon occurring when Danish Lutherans, Finnish Lutherans, Swedish Lutherans, Norwegian Lutherans, and most German Lutherans waved to each other on their way home from their respective church services.

Interior Decoration Mint green paint, new linoleum, and a variety-pac of colored hymnals. (See **Controversy** and **Pictures**.)

Intermediary (See **Intercede/Intercession**.)

Introit Apparently, the opposite of Detroit.

Invite This is the new trend in Lutheranism. It used to be that one was invited to a wedding . . .

period. Now one is invited to teach Sunday School (vs. assigned), invited to membership (vs. asked to join), invited to pray (vs. told to do so without ceasing), and invited to fellowship (vs. show up or else). This, too, shall pass.

Iota House An Augsburg College campus house located smack-dab across the street from Murphy Square that housed 24 Lutheran women who got distracted from preparing themselves to be "educated for service" by Melvin Men and other men. (See **Zeta House**.)

Is It You, Then? A typical Norwegian Lutheran question that is to be answered with another question, like "Oh, are you in town too?"

Isolation Like a quarantine, but for lesser illnesses like when Jean couldn't go to Sunday School because she had ringworm and pinkeye.

It's Too Tomatoey A phrase uttered by Olaf Peterson every time his Mrs. asked him what he thought of the new tomato hotdish she made.

Ivory 1. What the missionaries home on furlough brought for Show and Tell and blew through. 2. A color that has implications. (See **Off-White**.)

Ivy 1. A kind of vine that grew along the south

side of the church steps. 2. What they put in Emma's arm when she was in with her gall bladder, but they spelled it differently.

J...

Jacob's Ladder A work of art immortalized by Augsburg Publishing House in Lutheran Sunday School books that looked like a common farm ladder only Jacob's was painted in pastels and didn't have chips in it, oil marks, or missing rungs.

Jail Something like the reformatories for boys at St. Cloud or Red Wing, MN, but for old men who had tasted too much devil's drink.

Jam 1. Homemade fruit preserves that sell well at the Harvest Festival and cover up the holes in the homemade bread. 2. What Alma Auguston got into when she told Mavis Mortensen that the Ringstad girl was "p.g." 3. A part of the basement window that is spelled with a silent "b" on the end. 4. A word that describes how sardines are packed into a tin, and how Lutherans are packed into the church basement for *lutefisk* suppers. 5. A kind of "session" that Augustana College called its fall hootenanny so it would sound more worldly to the fresh-men. 6. Regardless of meaning, a word that is pronounced "yam" by Scandinavian Lutherans. (See **Immaculate Conception**, **Necking**, **Yam**, and **Yoke**.)

Janitor The "Elmer's Glue" of every local congre-gation who looked scary, but deep down loved kids and sweeping up rice.

January The time of the year on the church calen-dar when Lutherans are so crabby and gloomy that they might as well have the Annual Congregational Meeting, i.e., "It can't get much worse."

Jar 1. Something made by Mason and Ball which Lutheran women filled with sauce. 2. A word to describe Gertrude Severson's nerves and ribs after she drove her Edsel through the cemetery fence, as in "Ya, she sure was jarred up some, then."

Java Heathen coffee that comes from somewhere in the Pacific near Borneo.

Jealous What, according to Luther, "our God is," but what we shouldn't be.

Jell-O Just a delivery system for fruit cocktail.

Jewels Clip-ons, popbeads, and FFA tie clips.

Job Depending on how one says it, what we were put on earth to do, i.e., a job! An example of what will happen to us if we don't do our job is Job, a man in the Bible, who had his material possessions taken away and replaced by boils. (See **Poultice**.)

John Deere Day A quasi-Lutheran holiday because all the women cook and all the Scandinavians attend.

Joints 1. Where Catholics can get crippled from too much beer. 2. Where Lutherans can get crippled from arthritis.

Judge and Jury What Helmer Huggerud decided he'd be when he took matters in his own hands and shot the neighbor's dog because he was pretty sure the dog was killing his chickens.

Judgement Day Something quite a bit tougher than 4-H Achievement Day or Public Questioning.

Juice Lemon stuff Scandinavian Lutherans put on fish so it won't taste so "fishy."

Jumper 1. One who enters the contest at the Annual Sunday School Picnic. 2. The ninth grade sewing project which was offset with long white stockings and a white blouse with a Peter Pan collar. 3. A kind of cable used in the winter to ensure that Lutherans have no excuse for skipping services.

Jungle 1. Where Otemba lived before the missionaries found him. 2. A kind of gym at the parochial school in town.

Junk Food Anything that isn't made from scratch.

Justice of the Peace A local official who performed the marriage ceremony for Lutheran girls who, most likely because of dancing, had a "bun in the oven" and no shame. (See also **Begat**.)

Justification Herein lieth the essence of Lutheranism. Read about Martin Luther on your own.

K...

K.P. An abbreviation at Bible Camp for "kitchen patrol" which translated into setting the tables for 150, dishing up and serving the food, clearing the tables and washing them down with bleach, putting the food away, washing and drying the dishes, putting the dishes away, sweeping and washing the dining hall floor, getting up half an hour before everyone else and eating cold leftovers. This is not to be confused with P. K. which was short for "preacher's kid." P.K.s never had K.P.; they were too busy practicing piano and cornet for the Friday night talent show.

Keep it to Yourself This is right up there in the Lutheran lexicon with 'This Is Most Certainly True!', 'How Is This Done?', and 'What Does This Mean?' Although it wasn't written down in the Catechism, we're pretty sure it originated with Martin himself. 'This Is Most Certainly True!'

Kept Woman A borderline Lutheran who didn't do any more than expected and got by with it.

Kerchief A little thing that Paul used in the 'Book of Acts' to heal those who were poorly and possessed with demons, and now Lutheran women wear them over their heads and ears to keep from getting poorly. Teenaged girls also wore them tied around their necks in the 50s to show that they were going steady, i.e., possessed.

Kerosene A fuel available to Lutherans before the REA came through that lit up churches, heated chicken coops and hog barns, and removed paint (and some skin) from hands and lice from hair.

Key 1. A device for opening the back kitchen door of the church that no one ever found. 2. A musical point of reference that some choir members never found.

Kickerinos A type of classy overshoe that Lutheran girls got as Christmas presents in the late 50s which were either black or gray and had fur that folded down around the ankle. When a Lutheran girl was knee-deep in snow, the fur became wet and left a black dye mark around the ankle that looked like a tattoo, but wasn't. These boots were commonly called "Kicks." When Barbara Lorseng's mother asked her why she called her boots "kicks,"

Barbara answered, "Just for kicks, I guess."

Kid A baby goat in the Bible. A baby Lutheran in church.

Kidney 1. A kind of bean that the Leaguers wanted in their chili after the sleighride. 2. A kind of stone that Oliver Gjermundson couldn't pass so the neighbors had to take over his fieldwork.

Kimono A silky kind of sashed dress that the missionaries brought back from Japan, and a fancy name given to an ordinary chenille robe by women who wanted to be fancier than they really were.

Kiss What Judas did to Jesus in Gethsemane which was bad, and what Sven finally did to Ida in the kitchen — after they'd been married four years — which was okay.

Kissing A way to transmit deadly germs to Lutherans unless they are confirmed; preferably engaged.

Kitchen With the exception of the sanctuary, this was the most important room in the Lutheran Church. This full-service room — which doubled as a Sunday School room — was equipped with cupboards that held salt and pepper shakers, sugar bowls, pressed glass pickle dishes, pressed glass round serving trays, water and nectar glasses, coffee cups, plates, butter plates, kettles, enameled coffee pots, nectar pitchers, potato mashers, LB and AAL napkins, dishtowels, dishrags, potholders, silverware, serving pieces, and places for table cloths, slop pails, mops, refrigerators, stoves, and work tables. The serving counter — which held a pressed pickle dish that was used for the free will offering — was where the real fellowship began. Kitchens were not equipped with chairs; only with two stools to sit on to butter buns. (See **Buck** and **Free Will Offering**.)

Knock What we stand at the door and do, and what Phillip Estavold's Buick did when he forgot to put in ethyl.

Kool-Aid The replacement for Watkins nectar which came out when carpets started replacing linoleum in church basements. Kool-Aid has more sugar than Watkins did and makes kids more hyper so they spill on the new carpet.

***Kraut* Suppers** These were to German Lutherans as *Lutefisk* suppers were to Norwegian Lutherans; a time of good ethnic food and fellowship, but a fundraiser in disguise.

Kum-Ba-Yah A song that Lutheran children learned from foreign missionaries and sang at Bible

106

Camp. It was the first African song that Lutherans learned to sing, and the only other African stuff they could say was "Otemba" and the Swahili version of "*I will make you fishers of men*," but they didn't learn to spell it. Phonetically it was something like "Peska dory ya ho sa day, ya ho sa day, ya ho sa day," . . . you get the drift.

L...

Label What we were supposed to do to sauce jars and cakepans, but not do to people.

Labor 1. Toil and work that has moved out of the vineyards and into the wheat, oats, barley, bean and cornfields, into the garden, house, barn, and church. Sometimes one gets paid for it. 2. A kind of severe pain inflicted on women. They do not get paid for it; they pay <u>out</u> for the experience. (See **Dancing**.)

Lace 1. The kind of collar worn by sweet, little, elderly Lutheran women, and the kind of table-cloths that Lutheran women "use for best." 2. How a Scandinavian Lutheran pronounces "lays," as in "Ah, shoot. He just lace around the house all day." (It is grammatically incorrect, but a common expression.)

Lacking Moral Conviction A confirmed Norwegian Lutheran girl who goes to services at the German Lutheran Church across the street because most of the boy's basketball team goes there. (See **Parochial**.)

Ladle A handy utensil for dishing up soup and for scooping melted butter on potatoes and *rømmegrøt*.

Ladylike What little Lutheran girls are supposed to dress and act like after age five.

Lame Brain The offspring of a mixed marriage. (See **Half-Breed**.)

Lame Duck 1. The minister during the month before his farewell sermon. 2. An animal that Alf Knutsvig was left with when the rendering truck driver backed up without looking.

Lamentations A Book in the Bible that could have been written by Scandinavian Lutherans who know what Lent is really all about. (See **Lutheran**.)

Lamp A little thing about the size of a half-used roll of toilet paper that sits above the music on the organ and kills the atmosphere at a Candlelight Service.

Land of Promise The Red River Valley.

Languages Danish, Finnish, Norwegian, Swedish, Icelandic, German, Hebrew, Greek, and broken English.

Lanky What all the Lindquist boys were.

Lap 1. Kind of like padded pews that grown-ups have for little kids to sit on during services, some more padded than others. 2. A portion of a race that town boys run wearing short-shorts. 3. What cats do to milk, and Scandinavian farmers do to coffee on a saucer.

Lap Robes What the Martha Circle makes for shut-ins. (See **Homebound**.)

Lard An insulating product with a high "R" factor that is also the "Elmer's Glue" in all Scandinavian Lutheran white foods. (See **Insulation**.)

Large A proper adjective for the portions of food — and the proportions of women — in the Lutheran Church Basement kitchen.

Latecomer Someone whose cows got out just before church services started, not to be confused with a "Johnny-Come-Lately" which is a late bloomer like the Larson boy whose voice didn't change until after he was confirmed.

Latin A Catholic language. (See also **Languages**, *Agnus Dei*, *Excelsis*, and *Gloria Dei*.)

Law 1. Something that got started with Moses and gets added to each day by many Lutherans. 2. What Stephen Nelson — who doesn't want to farm — is studying in college, and it's not the first five Books of the Old Testament, either. 3. What most farmers call the game warden, as in "Here comes the Law."

Lay Preacher This is a word meaning "without a collar." Lay preachers stand and sit and drink coffee just like ordained pastors do.

Lazy Susan This is not found in a Lutheran Church Basement; pressed glass pickle dishes are.

Lead Depending on how it is pronounced, this is either what breaks on pencils at Sunday School, or what the pastor tries to do to his flock.

League The last name of Luther and Walther, sort of cousins who belonged to different synods like the Preuses.

Leap of Faith What the church council takes when it expects the old coal furnace to make it through another winter.

Leapfrog A game that Lutheran girls couldn't play at VBS recess because they didn't wear pants. (See **VBS**.)

Learn it by Heart A Lutheran phrase for "memorize all of this and don't blow it or you might not get confirmed!"

Leave 1. A contemporary word for "furlough." 2. A verb used frequently by big sisters, as in "Quit snooping and leave me alone, you pest!"

Leaven An Old Testament word like "circumcision" that was read in church, but never used in daily conversation. (See **Circumcision**.)

Lecture What the pastor gave to Herman and Melvin who were caught stealing sugar lumps from the church kitchen cupboards.

***Lefse* Day** The day after everyone gets together to peel. A day of flipping and turning and rolling and folding, and we're not talkin' laundry. It is held two days before the Annual *Lutefisk* Supper so one isn't too pooped out for the big day, and it's an unusual day regarding attendance because either too many show up and just get in the way, or not enough show up and the same old few get stuck with all the work. Old aprons, sensible shoes, and hairnets are appropriate attire.

Lefse **Turner** 1. Something that looks like a yardstick with *rosemaling* on it that is used to flip the *lefse*. 2. The Lutheran woman who uses the turner is also the turner, but she isn't *rosemaled*, just a little Lady Esther face powder, rouge, and rose water. (See **Rose Water**.)

Left-Wing The kind of people who worked on the Green Hymnal. (See **Featured Speaker**, **Free Thinker**, and **Support Group**.)

Leftovers The *lutefisk* bones and Mrs. Julia Ruud's watermelon pickles.

Legacy What Johannes Kvile left behind. (See **Quarter**.)

Legend A story that gets passed down from the fathers to the children of the third and fourth generations, like the one about Albert Heskin's sow that got bred too early in the season and had 21 piglets in early March out in North Dakota in a drafty barn in Traill County, and they all got pneumonia and died, all 21 of them! Otherwise, everyone was sure it would have been a world record — 21 piglets in one litter.

Legion 1. The name of a demon in the New Testament who was filled with evil spirits. 2. The name of a club in town where one can pay to get filled with evil spirits.

Legitimate 99.64 percent of Lutheran children.

Leif Ericsson A Lutheran Viking who had "turned," and who brought some Danes and Norwegians to America to carve a few rocks and pick up some grapes on the East Coast because everything, including the gooseberries, had been picked clean in Iceland. (See **To Turn**.)

Leisure Time This is not a Lutheran phrase.

Lemonade A simple, refreshing drink served in the summer at Ladies Aid, but it gets a little more complicated in Lemmon, SD where the Ladies Aid is called the Lemmon Aid.

Lent 1. Forty days of the year when non-Scandinavians get somber and reflective and think dark thoughts just like the Scandinavian Lutherans do all 365 days of the year. 2. Past tense of "lend" that's rarely used correctly. Usually folks just say, "I loaned you a buck last year," or even "I borrowed you a buck." Tsk, tsk.

Leper Colony A place overseas where sick people unroll the bandages that Lutheran women rolled up. (See **Rolling Bandages** and **Service Projects**.)

Let Me Do It (See also **I'll Dry**.)

Level-Headed A Swedish Lutheran man who has *snus* running down both sides of his mouth. (See **Snuff**, definition #1.)

Leviticus A Book in the Bible that lets lifetime Lutherans point fingers and say, "Ya, I told you so!"

Lewd Tattoos, Dancing, Slinky, etc.

Liberal (See **Left-Wing** and its cross-references.)

Licking 1. What mother's helpers liked doing to spatulas. 2. What mothers gave their kids if they were caught putting that spatula back in the bowl.

Lie 1. A fib, like what Orval told his parents when they asked him where he'd been after Free Show and didn't get home until 20 minutes after the drawing was over. (Fibs can cause a kid to get sent to bed without supper.) 2. To plop down on the bed, as in " Go lie down before I really give you something to cry about!"

Lifelong Helpmeet Any kind of Lutheran spouse.

Lighten Up A phrase heard in Lutheran homes referring to a fresh coat of paint, not to one's mental status.

Lilacs A Lutheran flower used for Confirmation and Graduation doings and for May showers, weddings, anniversaries, and funerals. The other 11 months of the year the same aroma could be achieved through various toilet waters and dusting powders, which got especially powerful at Ladies Aid meetings when election of officers was being held.

Limelight What Arlys Arneson was in when she was crowned 4-H Health Queen at the County Fair. "I felt just like a goldfish in a bowl by a lava lamp," she said.

Limit 1. A kind of law dealing with maximums that is easier to pass than enforce, such as "You can only get three Northerns, two ducks, one buck, and four pieces of *lefse* per person per day. 2. When you can sense that your father is getting near the end of his rope, as in "You're pushing my limit now. You know the cows can't wait." 3. What the immigrants thought the sky was.

Limp 1. What Elvira Severson walked with for six weeks after her spikes got caught in the church's furnace grate when she was going up for communion at her sister's church in Altoona, IA. (See **Liniment**.) 2. The kind of dishtowels that were heaped on the counter after the Harvest Festival dishes had been done.

Line 1. A verb for how we stood after Opening Exercises as in, "Line up quietly now and pass to your Sunday School classes." 2. What Home Ec teachers wanted you to do with the skirt you were making. 3. A noun for what Widow Snustad had a bunch of on her forehead. 4. A mark on the playground that separated the boys from the girls.
5. A type of dancing done by cowboys in Medora, ND who were so busy rounding up cattle they forgot their Confirmation vows.

Lineage Something that had to do with the House of David at church, and with *Hallings* and *Sognings* at *lag* meetings.

Liniment What Elvira Severson put on her ankle the whole winter after her visit to Altoona. (See **Carbo-Salve**, **Limp**, and **Watkins**.)

Linen What the dead people in the Bible were wrapped up in, and a kind of girdle that Jeremiah encouraged Lutheran women to spend good money on, as in Jeremiah 13:1.

Line of Duty The hierarchy in the church basement kitchen that is put into place for all functions based on age, experience, number of small children at home, sense of detail, and degree of arthritis.

Lingo 1. A special kind of language the pastor

used that was hard to understand and had to do with trespassing. 2. A special language Finnish Lutherans used wherein they made "b" sound like "p". It could be heard in the Finnish Apostolic Lutheran kitchen when the women were preparing lunch for a funeral, and the top one in the line of duty would say, "Time to get b(p)usy now girls, and b(p)e on the b(p)all!"

Lingonberry A special Swedish treat that looked like a chokecherry, but tasted like heaven. (Apparently, it was too colorful for Norwegians because they never ate it at church.)

Link A part of a German Lutheran *bratwurst* or a part of the cemetery fence, both designed to keep the dead stuff in.

Lips A word that is only used in Lutheranism when one is talking about something that is chapped.

Lipstick An item so frivolous that Lutheran girls couldn't wear it until they were confirmed, and rarely wore it after they were married.

Liquid The kind of diet the doctor put Helmut Schmidtz on when he had such bad problems with liver spots.

Liquor The kind of liquid that gave Helmut Schmidtz the liver spots in the first place.

Listen Anglo-Saxon word for "now pay attention."

Litany A kind of Lutheran prayer with choral responses, and the whole series of medical problems that were plaguing Gunda Rasmussen from gout to spells to vapors to bursitis to ringworm to pinkeye to shingles to liver spots to swollen ankles to being just plain tuckered out, probably from reciting this litany to everyone she met.

Literal Interpretation For example, "Oh, I have a frog in my throat!" (See **High Church/Low Church**.)

Litter 1. Having a whole bunch of offspring at once, but used loosely as in, "Ya, those Catholics down the road. They have a whole litter of kids." 2. A kind of bug responsible for throwing cardboard boxes, beer bottles, busted up tire chains, and older fender-skirts in the ditches.

Little Red Chairs The nicest thing the church council did to make little Lutherans feel welcome at Sunday School.

Loafers 1. People, like bankers, who quit work too early in the day. 2. A kind of shoe-wallet combination that high school boys wore to church to keep their coins in.

Lo and Behold Something you say when you stand at a door and knock, and an acceptable Lutheran slang term used to express great excitement, as in "Lo and Behold, there he was storming down the road barefoot like a chicken with its head cut off and the bull was right on his tail!" (See **Literal Interpretation**.)

Local Color What Lutherans say the trees provide in October, and the gypsies on the old Korsgrund place provide the rest of the year.

Locket 1. What girls wear around their necks to hide their boyfriend's picture in. 2. What mothers in a hurry ask their kids about the door, "Didya locket?"

Lock-In A modern method of getting kids to stay in church.

Lock-Up What cops do to kids who don't stay in church.

Lodge 1. What Sons of Norway members belong to. 2. What the wheat does after a big thunderstorm.

Logical One of the bigger words Lutheran parents like to use, as in "Well, doesn't it seem logical to you that if you're gonna eat, you gotta work?"

Loin 1. Something the minister told us to "gird," but we didn't know where it was, or what "gird" meant either, so we just listened. 2. A kind of cloth never seen in the Johnson Store or in Sears-Roebuck. 3. A part of a pig.

Long Johns 1. A kind of pastry town men eat at the restaurant in town. 2. A kind of underwear farm men wear ten months of the year.

Long-Range Planning What the young seminarian wanted the church council to do when things were going just fine anyway.

Long-Winded A kind of preacher of the Swedish Lutheran persuasion in the Black Hymnal era.

Loopy 1. A kind of necklace worn by Lutheran women in the Roaring 20s with chemise dresses. 2. The Olufson boy.

Loose Women 1. Women who live in town, go bowling, read movie magazines, don't own property, and wear slinky clothes. 2. The Nidaros Ladies Aid women when they tried to round up Thompson's cows that had gotten out.

Loot A word Lutherans use to describe the goods in the candy and peanut sacks given out at the Annual Sunday School Christmas Program, and the money a Confirmand could be expected to get for Confirmation, as in "What ya gonna do with your loot?"

Lot 1. Abraham's nephew whose wife was a salty little thing who didn't follow directions too well. 2. A hunk of the cemetery you can buy ahead of time. 3. The amount of hairspray Southern Baptists use.

Lounge 1. A swanky public place where women can powder their noses, and a scuzzy public place where hard liquor is served. 2. A verb, followed by "around," for what town women did in the afternoons by the T.V. set next to a box of chocolates.

Love The predominant virtue in the Christian life that Lutherans could sing about, but got a little nervous talking about.

Low 1. The kind of "high" heels female Confirmands wore. 2. What the cattle did in 'Away in the Manger.'

Low Church Something that has more to do with liturgy than either geography or height. (See **High Church**.)

Lump 1. A verb as in what you could do with the preschoolers at Sunday School, i.e., "Lump them all together." 2. A noun for something that shouldn't be there, as in Mrs. Overlee's gravy, or as in "She gets a lump in her throat every time Marvin sings 'The Ninety and Nine.'"

Lust Misplaced desire.

Lutefisk **Supper** The highest Feast Day in the Norwegian Lutheran Church Calendar year.

Luther League An excuse to get out of the house on a school night.

Lutheran Someone who lives Lent all year long.

Lutheran Recreation Shuffleboard, greased watermelon contests, Drop the Hanky, blowing marshmallows across the table, Wink 'em, horseshoes, Hide the Thimble, Sunday afternoon naps, and Button, Button, Who's got the Button? (See **Activities** and **Games in the Basement**.)

"Lutheran Standard" A standard magazine for standard Lutherans that was published before a lot of mergers and splits when Lutheranism was pretty much standard. (See **Mergers and Splits**.)

Lye 1. The poison that cod is soaked in to make

lutefisk. 2. Abbreviation for the Lutheran Youth Encounter (LYE) teams that came to small rural churches to "witness." (See **Special Offerings**.)

M...

Maiden Name (See **Free Thinker**.)

Malice Twin sister of Alice Torgrimson who wasn't quite as nice.

Manger A word that used to be heard in reference to the place in the barn where we dropped hay for the cows, but with the advent of feedlots and the Green Hymnal, a manger is only found now in the Bible and at the church at Christmas time.

Manna White stuff that falls from heaven that is softer than hail.

Manners Another thing (along with parents, adults, the Bible, etc.) that little Lutherans had to mind.

Map of Africa A big piece of paper in the Sunday School room that had red thumbtacks (to indicate where the mission hut schools were located) with strings attached leading back to churches in the Midwest (to indicate where the pupil's pencils and soap bars had come from.)

Marble 1. Columns in the Catholic Church. 2. Cake in the Lutheran Church. 3. What Otto Paulson seems to have lost.

Masquerade *Juleboking* to Norwegian-Lutherans.

Meanings Martin Luther never said anything he didn't mean or couldn't explain. He was very orderly. (See **Order** and **How Is This Done?**.)

Measles A disease that little Lutherans got and they were pretty sure it was the early stages of leprosy. (See **Leper Colony**.)

Meat 1. The substance of a Lutheran sermon. 2. What Catholics had to abstain from on Fridays. (See **Sermon**.)

Meat on the Bones 1. What you want to make sure there is if you are serving a chicken dinner. (See **Butcher**.) 2. What Lutheran bachelors are looking for in a woman, as in "She's not hefty enough. She doesn't have any meat on the bones."

Medora Musical One of the few remaining places

you can bring the whole Lutheran family — from buntings to bed jackets — for wholesome entertainment. (There is some dancing, but it is done by clean-cut kids who know where to draw the line, even though they dance in hymnal-red shoes.) Call 1-800-Medora-1. (See also **Line**.)

Membership This is a word like fellowship that was, and really is, a noun but has become a trendy verb in trendy Lutheran churches that have liturgical dances, as in "You are invited to membership." Real Lutherans know that you are invited to join or to become a member. (See **Fellowship**.)

Mementos Wedding napkins, nut cups, placemats, name cards, funeral folders, and special bulletins that are kept forever just in case.

Memorize What identifies Lutherans from other faiths.

Memory Work The emphasis is on "work."

Mergers and Splits This is a special Lutheran phenomenon wherein individuals, congregations, and synods will split up over any number of things and then either recreate a similar organism, or merge with another of like or unlike quality. It is actually quite similar to the biological process of mitosis or even parthenogenesis, wherein a cell or unit can split and divide and become a new cell or unit. This process, parthenogenesis, is loosely translated as "virgin birth." Therefore, perhaps Lutherans see merging and splitting as a religious action. (See **Hymnal Committee**.)

Methuselah A guy in the Bible who lived to be 969 years old, the exact age that Willie Bolstad, the janitor, said he felt like after cleaning up the church after the Annual *Lutefisk* Supper.

Middle Ages 1. Many years A.D. when most people were Catholic and soap was scarce. 2. The span of years in a person's life that gets later and later as the person gets older and older.

Minister 1. Same thing as a pastor without his robe on. 2. A verb for what he is supposed to do to "his flock."

Missionaries Walking 'National Geographics' who exposed us to things we had never heard about, showed us R-rated slides, and got us all excited to be missionaries ourselves someday.

Model Lutherans The pastor's family.

Moderation in All Things The Lutheran "Golden Rule" applicable to absolutely everything from sleep to nuts and mints. (See **Nuts and Mints**.)

Modesty The Lutheran virtue that is easiest to pull off.

Mogan David The only kind of wine that Lutherans can pronounce and drink with a clear conscience.

Mold 1. The greyish-green stuff in the church basement that smelled. 2. What we are supposed to try to do in His image. 3. Round, bronze-colored things that Jell-O was made in for fancy occasions.

Monogram The red fingernail-polished initials on the cakepan. (See **Cakepan** and **VBS**, definition #2.)

Monuments The only place these were found in Lutheran Churches were outside in the cemetery.

Moody Bible Institute Where people with fluctuating hormonal levels must go.

Morgue A fancy name for "funeral parlor" used only on T.V., and only in connection with murder.

Morning Circle The group of Lutheran women most prone to hotflashes and spells brought on by the noonday heat.

Mothballs A ball smaller than a kittenball, not as good smelling as a meatball, looks like a faded lemon drop, and designed to keep members of the opposite sex away from one's clothes.

Mother's Day The Sunday when you could finally give her the marigold that you planted from seed in a paper cup at Sunday School in February.

Mountaintop Experience
What Moses had that Bible Campers have been trying to duplicate ever since.

Movies 1. The Ten Commandments.
2. Song of Norway.
3. Martin Luther (in black and white.)

Mrs. Jones This is someone everyone had to "wisit" after too much egg coffee. (See **Visit**.)

Mucilage A kind of Sunday School glue that comes in a bottle with a rubber cap. Little Lutheran girls use these bottles, when empty, as baby bottles for their dolls.

Mumble What you shouldn't do with your Christmas piece. (See **Pieces**.)

Murky 1. The contents of the 'Book of Revelation.' 2. The cistern water at Eksjø Danish Lutheran Church in Copenhagen Township, WI. (See **Cistern**.)

Music Something Lutherans are better at than most people.

Mustache The orange upper lip on all the VBS kids from the Watkins nectar. (See **Spit**, **VBS** and **Watkins**.)

Mustard 1. A seed talked about in the Bible. 2. What high school boys put on their hot dogs at the Annual Sunday School Picnic. 3. A plant that farm kids got paid to pull up, two cents for each hundred plants, but it was a good time to practice memory work and to ponder those less fortunate who didn't have real work.

Mutate (See **Mergers and Splits**.)

Myrtle 1. A plant in the Bible. 2. The third grade Sunday School teacher who all the boys called "Myrtle the Turtle" because she didn't have much of a neck.

Naked What heathens in 'National Geographic' were, and what Lutheran women who didn't have their good girdle on felt like.

Namesake Most Lutheran children's second name was that of their namesake. It wasn't a name most Lutheran parents would have chosen, but out of duty and sensibility, most Lutheran children had a namesake.

Nap on Sundays What Lutheran adults did on Sunday afternoon after services and dinner, and before company came to visit, eat lunch, and look at the fields.

Napkins What L B and AAL donated to Lutheran Church Basement kitchens hoping that members would reciprocate by buying life insurance policies.

Narrow-minded Stubborn Lutherans of the

Haugean persuasion. (See **Hans Nielsen Hauge**.)

Nationality Norwegian-American Lutheran, Swedish-American Lutheran, Danish- American Lutheran, Finnish-American Apostolic Lutheran, Icelandic-American Lutheran, and German-American Lutheran.

National Lutheran Choir A collection of Lutherans specializing in F. Melius who had grown up singing in church and college choirs and needed to get together with other Lutherans who could sing better than most of the members of their own church choirs. (See **F. Melius**.)

Nativity A manger scene complete with animals, wisemen, shepherds, and the Holy Family which was sometimes set up outside the church, but always inside the church during the Christmas season. A Lutheran nativity scene didn't put any special emphasis on Mary.

Natural Foods Meat and potatoes, *lutefisk* and *lefse*, bread and butter, and any other normal foods that were made with lard.

Naughty What little Lutheran boys were before they got confirmed.

Nazarene A name of a religious group whose

belief system was somewhere in between Wesley Methodists and Baptists.

Nazareth A place in the Holy Land where Jesus grew up that some Lutherans can find on a map. (See **Holy Land**.)

Near-Beer A beverage that looks like beer and tastes like beer, but isn't full of alcohol. Even so, Lutheran women don't like it, and prefer their men to drink coffee or lemonade.

Neat as a Pin A phrase used to describe Lutheran Fititude women whose clothes never look wrinkled even after they stand up after sitting through the whole sermon.

Neck Ring Thin bands of dirt that Norwegian Lutheran farm men always had in their neck creases, especially during harvest. Some Norwegian bachelor farmers weren't the best at cleaning up and their necks always looked gray.

Necking An unhealthy activity that made Mrs. Snustad justified in saying, "No wonder she's p.g.; they're always necking."

Nectar A sweet syrup that you mix with water and serve to children at church. Watkin's orange or cherry was the standard drink.

Nei The Norwegian-Lutheran way to say "no."

Needle and Thread Emergency supplies that every Lutheran woman carries in her purse, especially to a daughter's wedding and the Annual Sunday School Christmas Program.

Nerves of Steel A phrase to describe a Lutheran who shingles church steeples.

Never-Failing This phrase refers to a bulwark, and a certain kind of boiled chocolate frosting. (See **Bulwark**.)

New Pastor's Wife The wife of a pastor who has been at a church less than 12 years.

Newcomer A person who has been a member of a Lutheran Church for less than 12 years and has no known relatives in the congregation.

Newfangled A phrase used to describe a new stove in the church basement kitchen that doesn't have a pilot light.

Nicene Creed A creed of the Lutheran Church that was said once in a while, but didn't have to be memorized like the Apostle's Creed.

Nickel A denomination of money that was tied in

the corner of hankies and given to the Sunday School collection.

Night Time Services Services in the Lutheran Church that were held during Lent, or when a visiting missionary or traveling evangelist was in town. Night time Services made a lot of Lutherans feel uneasy, especially if the meetings were held in tents.

Nip it in the Bud What you do to a Lutheran youth who is caught skipping Sunday School and reading girlie magazines in the drugstore on Sunday morning.

Noah The man in the Bible who was responsible for saving the mosquitos.

Noisy What Saturday morning Sunday School Christmas program practices were all about.

Normal Norwegian Lutheran farm folks who didn't turn, who didn't dance, who memorized all of 'Luther's Small Catechism', and preferred white food. 'This Is Most Certainly True!'

Norsk Being of Norwegian heritage. Usually it is synonymous with being Lutheran.

Norwegian Bachelor Farmers Norwegian-

American men who didn't marry, lived in the country, ate Spam and Dinty Moore Stew, and didn't spend money — except on *lutefisk* suppers, bib overalls, and flannel shirts.

Norwegian Lutheran Guilt A lifelong curse that all Norwegian Lutherans are born with. Like original sin, surgery, or environmental tampering, it can't be corrected.

Notion 1. A hunch that you figure you better act on, i.e., "I think I'll take a notion and go visit Hilda in the Home". Sometimes it was just a half a notion. 2. Sewing supplies that quilters and seamstresses could never get enough of such as needles, pins, ribbons, and buttons. (Sunday School children would take the buttons to play Tiddly Winks with, and take the thimbles to play Hide the Thimble.)

Novice A Catholic term that didn't pertain to Lutherans.

'Now I Lay Me' The second prayer memorized by a little Lutheran. The first was 'Come Lord Jesus,' and the third was 'The Lord's Prayer.'

Nuptials A word that means the same as a "Wedding Service." This word was used in the local newspaper because it just sounded more dignified, kind of like the word "betrothal."

Nursing School A practical place to send a Lutheran girl who didn't want to marry the neighbor boy, pack his lunches, and live on his homeplace.

Nuts and Bolts Since many of the members of a Lutheran congregation were farmers, a new pastor had to learn how to use words such as "nuts and bolts" when he was talking about putting some "meat" in his sermon. (See **Meat**.)

Nuts and Mints Unlike "nuts and bolts," these are condiments served at weddings, silver and golden wedding anniversaries, and at a church bridal shower given for the pastor's daughter or other fancy members. (Kids thought nuts and mints were the best part of the lunch.)

Nut House A place where Lutherans who couldn't "snap outta it" ended up.

Nylons A type of hose stocking (with seams up the back that were always crooked) that proper Lutheran women wore whenever they were out in public. Hoisted up by garter belts, they itched and ran and caused women to sweat more than usual. Old ones were made into rugs or chore boys, or used as for storing glad bulbs over the winter. (See **Chore Boy**, **Clear Fingernail Polish** and **Glad/Glads**.)

Obadiah A Book in the Bible that most Lutherans can pronounce, but can't tell you what it is all about.

Obedient Knowing enough not to sass or lip off to your parents, pastors, or anyone else in charge.

Obligation Things Lutherans have to do without complaining, like going through Public Questioning, taking sermon notes, sitting with an old maid at the mother-daughter banquet, and going to church every Sunday. In other words, Lutherans had to behave, act decent, not get their name in the newspaper, and turn out!

Off-the-Shoulder A type of dress that floozies wore that didn't belong in the Lutheran Church, even at a wedding when it was 105 degrees.

Offensive What *lutefisk* smells like to non-Scandinavians.

Office Closed This is a notice on local Lutheran Church calendars for every Monday. Do not schedule surgery or die on this day.

Officer What Lutherans elect for every organization in the church. The Ladies Aid had the most officers, but most organizations just had four.

Off-White The color a bride wore when things were suspect. (See **Ivory**.)

Okey-Dokey An American slang for "Ya, sure, you betcha."

Old Catholics Those Catholics who believed all Lutherans were going to hell. (See **Roman Catholic**.)

Old Country Norway, Sweden, Denmark, Iceland, Finland, and Germany.

Old Maids Things found in church pews, and in popcorn.

Ole 1. A cheap fraud when it comes to butter.
2. A good usher.

Opposites Attract When a Norwegian Lutheran

boy shines up to a Swedish Lutheran girl.

Order 1. This is a very important Lutheran word, and the main Lutheran virtue. Everything in one's life, home, church, community, cupboards, tool box, tackle box, drawers, closets, cubby hole, etc., should be in order. There is also an 'Order of Service' even though it varies from Sunday to Sunday, and from Lutheran Church to Lutheran Church. 2. This is also a Lutheran verb that has plagued Sunday School superintendents for decades: "Did you order enough Sunday School materials? Why did you order so many for the kindergarten class? Why does the order cost so much? Why didn't you order it earlier?" And on and on and on . . . . (See **Annual**).

Ordination A Service and Rite of passage which made the neighbor boy into a bona fide minister and gave him the privilege of living rent-free in a parsonage.

Organ Whether it be a pipe or a Hammond, it is the only true Lutheran musical instrument that is needed in the church.

Organist The lady who played the music in church. Sometimes she played on a pipe organ, sometimes she played on an electric Hammond, sometimes she was daydreaming, sometimes she did a pretty good job, and often she was the pastor's wife. Even though most Lutheran Church organists were very diligent and played for 30-40 years, most weren't as good as Steve Gabrielsen. 'This Is Most Certainly True!'

Orthodox Those who believe that one shouldn't be able to tell — either by the lunch or the sermon — whether one is attending a wedding or funeral in the Lutheran Church.

Otemba The name of a character in a book about a heathen child who turned Christian. This book was usually given to Sunday School children as a reward for perfect attendance, or as a gift from their teacher at Christmas.

Outcasts Those who are buried outside of the Lutheran cemetery gates for one iniquity or another.

Outdo What Lutheran Church Basement Women try to do in regards to the height of their angel food cakes as compared to other women's cakes.

Outlook This has to do with the weather forecast for the Annual Sunday School Picnic or the Annual *Lutefisk* Supper.

Outside the Faith Anyone who hadn't memorized 'Luther's Small Catechism.'

Overalls Outer garments that men didn't wear to church unless they were fixing something at church during the middle of the week, or digging a grave.

Overflow A place for the Christmas or Easter crowd to sit. Sometimes it is needed on Confirmation Sundays if there is a big class, like more than five.

Overshoes Black rubber buckle contraptions that fit over shoes and were worn in the church and the barn. Midwest Lutheran men always lost them, left them, or got them mixed up with other Lutheran men's rubbers at Brotherhood. (See **Brotherhood**.)

Ox An animal we shouldn't covet. (See **Bulwark** and **Covet Thy Neighbor's Ox**.)

Oxfords Sensible black or brown tie shoes that Lutheran women wore when they got "down to business" in the church basement.

Oxymoron 'Luther's <u>Small</u> Catechism.' 'This Is Most Certainly True!'

Pacifier An attention-getter such as making a mouse out of a hanky to keep little children from fidgeting in church. (See **Fidget**.)

Pack Rat A Lutheran woman who saves everything because she would feel guilty throwing out things that people in Formosa or Madagascar might be able to use someday. Things such as old high heels, rusty zinc lid covers, eggshells, string too short to save, and anything with religious themes like old church bulletins, napkins from weddings, tracts, obituary announcements, and church annual reports dating back to the 30s.

Pagan Dancing, drums in church, and Lutheran women who look like painted ladies and wear big dangly earrings and spike heels to church.

Pale as a Ghost The color Serena Beate turned when she found out that her son was thinking about "turning". (See **To Turn**.)

Palm Sunday The Sunday before Easter when Lutherans in the Red River Valley and parts of Wisconsin got to sing 'The Palms' in church. (Red River Valley Lutherans didn't wave branches until after the Green Hymnal was introduced.)

Paltry The amount of hotdish that frail widows bring to a funeral.

Pamphlet Little brochures that were written to entice Lutherans to go to Bible Camp. With phrases like, "The air-conditioning comes right off the lake," any kid who was out baling hay and picking rocks was won over.

Pan of Bars An 11 x 14-inch pan of cake-type dessert that was always needed for Lutheran Church Basement functions. Bars — unlike cake brought by town women — were always homemade.

Pantaloons A type of garment that looked like a slip and felt like a slip, but it was a slip with legs in it. Lutheran girls wore them under skirts in the early 60s, but these weren't like Little Bo Peep's who was always slippin', and these weren't itchy like a 50-yard Alice Long cancan either. (See also **Cancan** and **Petticoat**.)

Pantry Panties It's not what you think! These are elasticized plastic covers that fit over bowls of leftovers.

Panty Girdle A contemporary girdle with legs in it. Even though some still had garter belts attached, they felt a lot more modern, that's for sure.

Papers Things we brought home from Sunday School that had gold, blue, or red stars on them.

Parchment A type of paper that Baptismal Certificates were written on, and a paper used to line fancy cakes that were served at teas when past pastors' wives were visiting for a church anniversary celebration.

Paring Knife A handy knife that veteran potato peelers used when peeling potatoes for *lutefisk* suppers. Unskilled workers used a potato peeler so they wouldn't waste so much.

Parish What Catholics called the church. The only time Lutherans talked about a parish was when they were referring to a Parish Education Building. A Parish Education Building was a new building that was connected to churches that were tired of holding Sunday School classes in the furnace room.

Park The town playground where town Lutheran churches held the Annual Sunday School Picnic. Country churches had their own park, i.e., the cemetery, and besides country kids could make their own fun.

Parlor Games Mild games that The Daughters of the Reformation and Young Missionary Society girls played at a year-end luncheon in the parsonage.

Parochial Primary and secondary education that is affiliated with a church body. German Lutheran parochial school kids attend these schools to learn how to play basketball so they can give the local town teams a run for their money. Catholics attend them so they can give money to pagan babies, and be sure to become lifelong Catholics. (Some parochial kids were quite wild.)

Parsonage A home where the pastor and his family lived. Like the Lutheran Church, the parsonage was considered a public building. Sometimes Lutheran Church Basement Women housecleaned the parsonage if the pastor's wife didn't keep it up to snuff. (See **Snuff**.)

Partake What Lutherans did at Communion and at *Lutefisk* suppers.

Partiality A type of treatment that the pastor's daughter received when the Sunday School committee was deciding who would play the part of Mary in the Annual Christmas Program.

Partition Dividers, sometimes made out of bed-spreads, that were used to carve Sunday School rooms out of the big church basement.

Passed On Kicked the bucket, slept away, called home, checked out, didn't come out of a spell, etc.

Passion Week 1. This is a misnomer. Lutherans — especially Norwegian-American ones, were never passionate — and if they ever were tempted to be so, it certainly wouldn't have been during this week. (See also **Lent**.) 2. The week before Easter. The only time Lutherans went to church on Friday, but they could still eat meat! (See **Temptation**.)

Pastor A low church way of saving "Reverend."

Pastoral Duties that the pastor did grudgingly and ungrudgingly for his flock such as visiting Mrs. A. O. Romegaard when she was having her dizzy spells. This type of home visit included reading devotions, having a cup of coffee and a cookie, and listening to complaints about physical illnesses and about others in the congregation.

Pastor's Wife The woman who was always on display. She not only knew how to play piano, but she also had to be good at giving devotions, slow to anger, and abiding in steadfast love. She had to be dressed sensibly and modestly, and her kids had to be an example to everyone.

Patron Saint Martin Luther is the closest to what Lutherans would consider to be a patron saint. He stood for everything they believed in. Like he said, "Here I Stand, then."

Pavilion Dens of iniquity that were located near lakes and enticed young people to dance and stray.

Pay Respects The act of going to a funeral parlor to look at your friend lying in a casket, sign the guestbook, see who gave the bouquets of glads, read in the guestbook to see who has signed in, and beat it out of there before the immediate family sees you.

Peace A verbal command from the pastor telling you to shake hands with total strangers right in the middle of Sunday Morning Services. This behavior certainly didn't go on in the Black Hymnal era when things were normal. (See **Normal**.)

Peaked This was usually pronounced "peek-id." This was how some women looked when they were having a spell, and how some grooms looked when they were getting hitched. (See **Hitch**.)

Pedal Pushers A type of pants which covered the knees that Lutheran women wore in a pinch if a housedress didn't fit the bill. By the time these were worn out and put in a box for the missions, they usually were stained with beet and chokecherry juice. Lutheran women got a little nervous watching filmstrips of mission fields for fear that the pedal pushers they gave to the clothing drive might just show up on the screen.

Peel 1. Stripping a potato of its skin in order to scallop it or to make *lefse*. 2. A misspelling of the sound of ringing bells. 3. What the Tollefson boy does out of the parking lot when he is trying to impress hoods and other farm boys.

Pen Pal A friend made at Bible Camp who Lutheran youth would correspond with for about two weeks after they went home from camp. Bible Camp pen pals usually signed each other's autograph books, too.

Pennies What young Lutheran kids put in the birthday bank, junior high Lutherans put on a railroad track, teenage Lutheran youth put in their penny loafers, and older Lutherans save for a rainy day.

Pentecost The birthday of the church. After the

Green Hymnal came out, some congregations decorated the church on Pentecost Sunday with red balloons and geraniums. As Mrs. Snustad told Pastor A.O. Haugen early one May Monday morning, "Isn't anything sacred anymore? You would have thought the sanctuary was a circus tent, for crying out loud."

Peonies A type of white, pink, or magenta flower that was found on the Lutheran Church altar in early summer. Most Lutheran women raised peonies, so it was a good filler flower to use after the lilacs were gone and before the glads came into bloom.

Perfect Attendance The reason Lutheran children got certificates, Sunday School pins with a wreath encircling the pin, and second, third, fourth, fifth, and sixth-year bars which were added to the bottom of the pin. The Asiatic flu, scarlatina, and ringworm that went around in the late 50s kept many a Lutheran kid from getting a perfect attendance prize.

Perm Chemicals put out by Richard Hudnut that a Lutheran woman put on her hair to make it look Lutheran-coiffed.

Pester What boys do to girls in Sunday School. It rhymes with "fester" and has the same result, i.e., it aggravates, eats at you, gets worse, and seems to last forever. An example would be Lutheran parents asking their children, "Do you have your memory work done yet, then?" (See **Fester**.)

Petitions The 'What Does This Mean?' section of 'The Lord's Prayer' that Lutheran Confirmands were required to memorize and repeat back to their minister at Public Questioning. Some of the petitions were shorter and easier to memorize than others, so usually the boys got asked those.

Petrine Theology The theology found in the 'Book of James' that Catholics use to justify good works.

Petticoat These weren't coats at all, but rather undergarments made out of nylon or net that made Lutherans girls itch and squirm. (See also **Cancan** and **Pantaloons**.)

Pew A really hard bench that Lutherans sit on during services. Eight Lutherans in stormcoats — or ten Lutherans with summer church clothes on — can fit in one pew. (When it gets too humid, people's legs stick to the pew.) The back of the pews have racks to hold hymnals, but since the Green Hymnal came out, one can find pencils and scratch paper for Hangman and Tic Tac Toe in the pew racks, too. (This is in addition to the little bag/

activity kits that the ushers give to little kids so they don't have to pay attention.) Pretty soon there will be pillows and snacks put there, too. *Uffda!*

Pew Protocol Knowing who sits where in church is an etiquette code that Lutherans adhere to, unless one is a two-time-a-year Christmas and Easter Lutheran. Lutherans believe that having a regular pew is like squatter's rights, i.e., once you have been in a pew for so long, it is your pew.

Piano The official Lutheran instrument which sits in Lutheran Church balconies and basements, and always needs tuning. (See **Accompanist**.)

Pickles   Beets, watermelon, and cucumbers that had been preserved in brine and are brought to church for every meal to provide color and continuity to an otherwise bland meal. A Lutheran Church Basement meal without pickles would seem as naked as a Lutheran lady feels not wearing her good girdle on Sunday. (See **Chunky Pickles**, **Naked**, **Relish**, and **Good Girdle**.)

Pictures These were wall paintings of Bible scenes put out by Augsburg Publishing House that hung in every church basement, big painted pictures of angels or rocks painted by itinerant Norwegians for the altar in most Lutheran churches, and "Grace" and "The Lone Wolf" in Scandinavian-

American Lutheran homes, and one of George Washington in public school classrooms.

Pictorial Directory A soft-covered pictorial book showing color-coordinated Lutheran families dressed up in navy blue, red, and white — or hunter green, brown and beige — and touching.

Piece of Cake 1. Something everyone ate at Lutheran funerals, Ladies Aid meetings, and at weddings. 2. A slang term for something easy, like when the pastor asked a Confirmand at Public Questioning who Adam's wife was, the other Confirmands would think to themselves, "Man, that was a piece of cake."

Pieces 1. What all Lutheran children had to memorize for the Annual Sunday School Christmas Program. 2. The subject of much church basement discussion before funerals as in, "Well, if we don't know how many are coming, how big should we cut the pieces?" 3. Sections of cloth for quilts for the foreign missions.

Piecework Pieces of fabric that women sewed together for mission quilts. Because idle hands were the tool of the devil, doing piecework was one way Lutheran women could keep on the straight and narrow. (See also **Crochet**.)

Pierced Ears Heathen holes that don't belong in proper Lutheran ladies' ears.

Piety Hans Nielsen Hauge's brand of Lutheranism that was practiced in the Midwest. (See **Hans Nielsen Hauge**.)

Pillars 1. Poles that Lutheran kids would swing around when their parents would be drinking coffee and visiting in the Lutheran Church Basement. 2. Steadfast members who had sacrificed something. (See **Charter Member**, **Church Basement Poles**, and **Poles**.)

Pimiento A red, mild sweet pepper that is stuffed into green olives to provide the color at a Lutheran funeral lunch. One olive is cut horizontally into three pieces and placed on top of the Cheese Whiz that has been spread on diagonally-cut rye bread. (See also **Deadspreads**.)

Pin 1. Whether it was a safety, 'I am a Lutheran,' attendance, rolling, or hat pin — or even a *sølje* — pins were always an integral part of the Lutheran Church scene. 2. This can also be a verb, as in "Pin the diaper well;" or a verb to describe something that happens at state colleges, i.e., "The Smith girl got pinned." 3. Something even non-wrestlers wanted to do to someone, like "I'll see if I can pin him down."

Pitch Pipe A little gizmo used by *a cappella* male quartets and female triple trios to make sure they started out singing on the right note.

Pitcher Containers for nectar or water that were kept in a special cupboard in the Lutheran Church Basement, were usually made out of cheap thick glass, and lasted for generations.

Pizza Pie An Italian dish introduced to Luther Leaguers in the late 50s. Like *Sankta Lucia,* another Italian import, Scandinavian Lutheran youth enthusiastically embraced this Italian dish even though the older Lutherans didn't think much of it because it was too spicy and tomatoey. Like Hjalmer Larsson said to his brother, Emil, after trying pizza pie for the first time, "*Ish da*, this is spicy, and there is no cardamom in this stuff, to boot."

Plague In Biblical times God sent plagues such as frogs to punish the Egyptians. Modern Lutheran plagues are things like ringworm.

Plain Jane A wholesome Lutheran woman who wasn't much to look at, but could usually cook and clean and would have made a good "helpmeet" if she hadn't been so busy taking care of all the old people in her family. (See **Helpmeet** and **Lifelong Helpmeet**.)

Plaster of Paris A white material used for casting molds. Since Lutheran churches didn't have statues, they didn't have much use for plaster of Paris and just made things with Jell-O molds.

Plastic Newfangled material that was used for grave flowers and popbeads.

Plenary Indulgences This is Catholic theology. The only thing Lutherans indulge in are *lutefisk* suppers, and that's plenty good enough!

Plowshares The part of the plow that cuts the furrow. (We put this in so town Lutherans would know what were talking about.) It is also what the Bible says that we will turn our swords into, but Norwegian Lutherans gave up their swords after the Viking Era.

Plugged In What Lutherans did to hearing aids in the fourth pew from the back, and to coffee pots to blow fuses.

Plumbing Pipes that froze up which caused toilets to overflow. It was much less of a hassle when they used outhouses.

Plump The condition of many Lutheran Church Basement Women who had eaten too much *røm- megrøt,* delivered too many kids, and did too much tasting.

Poles 1. An ethnic group that was usually Catholic. 2. A supporting device for a Morton building roof. 3. In the Lutheran Church it was a recreational device and twirling around them was a close as Lutherans got to dancing. (See **Pillar** and **Church Basement Poles**.)

Politics in the Lutheran Church Hymnals, mergers, high church/low church and other problems discussed in the book, 'Growing Up Lutheran.' (See **Mergers and Splits**, **Hymnal Committee** and its cross references, and **High Church/Low Church**.)

Polyester A material that kept women away from the ironing board, but that heated the women up like an iron.

Polyesterfest A gathering of elderly women who are good at serving.

Pomegranate An exotic foreign fruit never served in the Lutheran Church even though it was mentioned in the Bible. It was probably bigger than a chokecherry, but the Sunday School teachers didn't go into detail.

Pondered This is what Mary did in her heart.

Pool Hall The den of the devil where hoods hung out.

Popbeads Plastic pull-apart beads that Lutheran girls wore so they could look like they came from the city.

Popcorn Prayer A spontaneous prayer that Lutheran youth had to say at Bible Camp. Most of them felt uneasy doing it.

Possessions Earthly things that got in the way of religion. (See **Earthly Possessions**.)

Postlude The closing music in the church service. Most Lutherans don't know what the word "postlude" means, but it's probably something like, "Finally I can go to the bathroom."

Potatoes What the Letnes Family raised in the Red River Valley. (The Letnes women always brought potato salad and scalloped potatoes to church doings.)

Potluck A meal where everyone brings something

to eat, everyone ends up eating too much, the scalloped potatoes melt the Jell-O, and there is always a nice variety. (See also **Fellowship Buffet**.)

Poultice A concoction made with dry mustard that draws matter and pus out of boils and other stuff that keeps kids out of Sunday School. (See **Fester** and **Job**.)

Pound How one weighs people, butter, and *lutefisk*.

Pour The art of dispensing coffee from a pot to people in line at weddings and other fancy doings. Usually the aunts who were a Lutheran wedding couple's godmothers pour at a wedding. At a "Silver," the one who pours always announces, "Just the cup, please." (See **Cup and Saucer**.)

Pout What Lutherans kids do when they look in their brown Sunday School Christmas bag and find more nuts than ribbon candy.

Power What the chairman of the Annual *Lutefisk* Supper felt when everything ran smoothly and they didn't run out of any food.

Practicing Piano What Lutheran kids did during their free time to get some culture.

Prayer 'Now I Lay Me,' '*I Jesu Navn*,' 'The Lord's Prayer,' and 'Come, Lord Jesus.'

Preach What preachers are supposed to do. Some can and some can't.

Preacher A man of the cloth who tries to lead a bunch of stubborn people. Sometimes he can and sometimes he can't.

Predestination The issue that keeps Presbyterians and Lutherans from merging.

Prelude A musical piece that the organist plays to get Lutherans out of the vestibule and into the sanctuary.

Premature (See **Necking**.)

Presbyterian (See **Predestination**.)

Present What Lutherans say instead of "Here" when roll call is taken.

Priest A Catholic name for a pastor.

Primal Scream Therapy Yelling "*Uffda!, Nei, Fyda!, Neiman, du da!,*" and "What in the World, then!" three times is about as primal as a Scandinavian Lutheran can get.

Proclaim What we are supposed to do with the Gospel. Norwegian Lutherans would rather people came to their senses on their own.

Produce 1. A noun for what Lutherans bring to the Harvest Festival if they haven't already canned it all. 2. A verb having something to do with the "begats." (See **Begat** and **Augsburg College**.)

Prodigal Son A Lutheran wayward son who spends the better part of his life in the cities, and then wants to come home and get part of the farm.

Programs Free entertainment at a Lutheran Church followed by lunch.

Protestant Followers of Martin Luther and other break-away groups from the Catholic Church. Nobody protests much now, unless it has to do with changing the hymnal color or merging with the Episcopalians.

Protestant Ethics Thou shalt work, wear suits to church, behave, act decent, turn out, and not get your name in the newspaper! 'This Is Most Certainly True!'

Provisions What Lutherans receive if they are willing to work hard enough.

Psalms The Book of the Bible that is considered the middle of the Bible. Most Lutherans can recite "the 23rd" by heart.

Psychiatry "Snap outta it," for crying out loud!

Publics A slang term for Lutherans used by Catholics, but not to our faces.

Public Drunkenness The ultimate shameful Lutheran behavior exhibited by the weakest of Lutherans. Whomever displayed this type of behavior didn't receive C.A.R.E. packages at Christmas either. (See **Baskets for the Poor**.)

Public Questioning A torturous night for Lutheran Confirmands when they stand in front of their minister, their families, and other interested Lutherans and answer questions the pastor fires at them at random. Some kids faint, other's throw up, and everyone is glad when it is over. 'This Is Most Certainly True!'

Pump Organ Shoes Flats.

Pumps 1. A type of organ in some Lutheran churches. Sometimes the organist's husband will pump from behind the organ, like at Waldheim Lutheran in North Dakota. 2. A type of shoe worn by some Lutheran women which often get caught in floor furnace grates when they go up for communion. 3. A type of activity associated with swings. A Lutheran child at the Annual Sunday School Picnic would beg his dad, "Pump me higher. Please, Dad, please?"

Pure 1. Good Watkins vanilla. 2. Good Lutheran girls, i.e., "Men don't marry public property." 'This Is Most Certainly True!'

Purse Strings A slang term used for the Ladies Aid Treasurer.

Push Up 1. False inserts that make a woman look like a streetwalker. (See **Hotdish.**) 2. Sherbet treats that used to cost a nickel. 3. What Lutheran women do to the wooden accordion divider window before serving church basement lunch.

Put on the Dog What Lutherans do on Easter Sunday, and fancy people try to do all year long.

Puzzle 1. A noun for cardboard pictures that are cut up into pieces and then put back together again by bored Lutherans. 2. A verb for how most Lutheran parents feel about their junior high kid's behavior.

Quack A pastor or his wife who try to promote ideas that are contrary to Lutheran ways of thinking as they have been taught for generations. For example, a pastor who says he personally doesn't see anything wrong with Lutheran youth doing the Bunny Hop or Snake Dance at Homecoming, better pack his bags quickly or go preach at the Congregational Church.

Quad A semi-enclosed outdoor area at Augsburg College that looked prettier in pictures than in actuality.

Quadruple What you do to glorified rice when you are making it for a big doings, like a Johnson funeral. (See **Quantity**.)

Quake What Confirmands do when they are grilled by the pastor at Public Questioning in front of everyone, including God. Shepherds did it, too, "at the sight" when they saw "glories stream from heaven afar."

Quality In Lutheran lingo this has to do with the "meat" in the sermon. (See **Meat**.)

Quantity A Lutheran word that has to do with food and the amounts that need to be prepared, especially for the pastor's daughter's wedding reception, or for a Johnson funeral. (See **Quadruple**.)

Quarrel How disagreements over the new hymnals always ended up.

Quarter 1. A generous Sunday School donation. 2. A generous piece of land donated by Johannes Kvile back in 1888 for the new immigrant church and a surrounding cemetery. (See **Legacy**.)

Queen of England A phrase used to describe a town woman who thought she was important, as in 'Who does she think she is anyway? The Queen of England?"

Question What Lutheran parents did to their kids every Saturday night in reference to their memory work. Also what Lutheran parents did to their youth when they came home from Luther League an hour after it was over.

Quilt 1. Something that occupies old maids' time and is sent to the mission field. 2. The most mis-spelled word in Lutheranism, usually spelled "guilt" — which then creates more.

Quintet A group of clean-cut, wholesome LBI students who came to perform at Sunday Night Services in small towns.

Rabble-Rousers Lutherans who are always trying to stir up the pot whether it's about hymnals, mergers, anniversary celebrations, stoves, or anything else that riles up one's neighbor.

Radical The President of Concordia College who allowed dancing to become legal. (See **Alumni**.)

Radio Ministry A favorite for $2.00 memorials in memory of departed Lutherans.

Rag Bag A bag that contains scraps that either go to the grease shed, or to the rug lady to weave.

Ragamuffin A Lutheran Sunday School student who always looked disheveled even at the Annual Sunday School Christmas Program.

Raiment The word for "clothing" that is used in the King James Version of the Bible.

Rain Bonnet A plastic covering Lutheran women carry in their purse, just in case. Sometimes called a "breeze bonnet."

Rally Day This does not have to do with car races. It is the first day of Sunday School in the Fall when nervous mothers, nervous first-time teachers, and polished little kids show up early and pretend they aren't nervous.

Ramshackle The way the Lutheran Church Basement kitchen looks after the Luther League has a pizza party.

Reading for the Minister This is what Scandinavian Lutherans called Confirmation class. However, this is a misnomer because Confirmands didn't <u>read</u> for the minister, they recited.

Reading Material Tracts, magazines, and pamphlets put out by Augsburg Publishing and other Christian publishing houses. Some Lutherans save reading materials for the shut-ins. Other Lutherans save reading materials just because they would feel too guilty to throw it out. (See also **Good Reading Material**.)

Reception From weddings to missionaries returning home on furlough, Lutherans have lots of receptions to attend. The pastor is given two receptions:

once when he comes to a new church, and once when he leaves. (That is, if he leaves in good standing.)

Recipe Written directions for making almost everything from chicken hotdish to homemade fly poison that were passed around Lutheran Churches like wildfire. (Some fancy town women wouldn't share their recipes.) Most Lutheran Churches sent their recipes to Iowa to get bound into a church cookbook that they could sell for money to remodel the church kitchen. Part of the cookbook proceeds often went to the mission field, also. (See **Fly Poison** and **Index**.)

Recitation What Lutheran kids did in Sunday School, Bible School, Bible Camp, and most of all, at Confirmation. (See **Memorization.**)

Reckoning To settle up the score. Just like everyone knows they have to reckon up their grocery bill at the end of the month or they won't eat, Lutherans know that when they've left this earth, they'll have to reckon up especially if they "turned" or didn't live by the 'Good Book.'

Records 1. The recording of everything from minutes of meetings to Baptisms, Confirmations, weddings, deaths, Sunday School attendance, what each member gave financially to church, who served when, and other valuable information. These were an integral part of every Lutheran Church. 2. What town kids played after school when farm kids were chorsing. (See **Chorsing**, **Home Visits**, and **Therapy**.)

Red Arms What Lutheran Church Basement Women had from mashing potatoes at *Lutefisk* suppers, not Communist military machines.

Red-Letter Days The practice of marking Holy Days in red letters on the Lutheran Church calendar. Red Letter days would include Confirmation Services, the Annual *Lutefisk* Suppers, Father-Son Banquets, Mother-Daughter Banquets, the Annual Church Cleaning Day, Sunday School Practice Days, and the Cemetery Association's Annual Meeting.

Red Shoes The color of shoes that Norwegian Lutheran women liked, but couldn't muster up the courage to wear.

Reformation Sunday The last Sunday in October which is set aside to honor Martin Luther and all the other renegades who stood up to the pope and said, "Enough's enough, then!"

Refreshments Food that is served in the Lutheran Church Basement which consists of bars and coffee. Refreshments are a lighter version of lunch, but more than coffee. For instance, refreshments would be served to the Church Council members at their monthly board meeting. One wouldn't go into a lunch format for so few people or at that hour of night.

Regular Someone who attends church every Sunday, gets to every Lenten Service, and attends all the special programs. A regular can be counted on to pay his fair share in *penger* and in hotdish donations besides being willing to serve on committees and teach.

Released Time A midweek booster shot of religion given during school hours. Lutheran kids would be hauled over to church to memorize, recite, and learn why they were put on this earth in the first place.

Relics 1. The rusty worn-out cars that were parked in the grove. 2. Venerated souvenirs associated with saints that Lutherans thought was just a bunch of *ingenting*.

Relief 1. This is what a bulletin provides to Lutheran women having hotflashes during services. 2. How Mrs. Snustad describes people who are too lazy to work, i.e., "They are on Relief." 3. An organization in the Lutheran Church that provides for

the truly needy is called Lutheran World Relief.
4. This is the feeling you have when you finally
find the bathroom in a different church.

Religious What Lutherans thought they should
be, Baptist felt they were, and Catholics were
taught that they were.

Relish 1. What a Lutheran woman did to corn
and cucumbers so she could bring more than pickles to the Mission Festival and other doings. 2. A
word sometimes used for "adoration," as in "Sylvia
just relished the senior boys." As Mrs. Snustad
said, "I don't know what's come over that girl anyway, but her mother had the same problems at that
age."

Remembrance Day A day to remember the dead,
visit their graves, honor the vets, and read the
names on the plaque at church of those members
who had died in the services — and we don't mean
the 10:00 o'clock Services, either.

Reminisce 1. Remembrances which were mostly
horror stories that older Lutherans told to their
children and grandchildren. These were stories
about reading for the minister in Norwegian or
German, stories about walking six miles and more,
. . . ya de da de da . . . , and stories about cold
outhouses. These stories were told so that the

180

younger Lutherans would become more thankful. It usually didn't work, though. 2. A magazine of the 90s that retired Lutherans like to read. (See **Reading for the Minister**.)

Render 1. To melt down fat from a butchered pig into lard to be used as an ingredient in homemade lye soap, flaky pie crusts, cookies, or "those good lard doughnuts." 2. A word used to describe the Peterson girl's ability to sing '*Hils fra meg der hjemme*' in perfect Norwegian at her grandparent's anniversary as in, "Last Sunday afternoon, Gloria Peterson, accompanied by her sister Elena, rendered a beautiful solo in the basement of First Lutheran in honor of her grandparent's 50th Wedding Anniversary. 3. To pay your taxes as commanded by the 'Good Book,' i.e., Render Unto Caesar, etc.

Rennet Tablets that Swedes bought at the drug store to make their beloved pudding at Christmas.

Renounce What Confirmands did at Confirmation. By renouncing the devil and all his works and all his ways, Lutheran Confirmands were pretty sure this included dancing, playing pool, and going to movies.

Repeat it Backwards and Forwards 'Luther's Small Catechism.' 'This Is Most Certainly True!'

Repertoire The list of musical works that the senior choir worked on for months and only performed twice.

Representative The LB or AAL insurance man who sells life insurance to you, drinks your coffee, and dunks your "yin-yer" snap cookies in your house while he is doing the paper work.

Request This follows the word "prayer" in new Lutheranism, and proceeds "your presence" on wedding invitations. Other than that, don't ask anything. Just do it yourself!

Rest 1. A musical term that Lutheran children learned about in junior choir. 2. What Lutheran adults did on Sunday afternoons.

Reunion A gathering of a collection of people — whether it be relatives or church friends or the third and fourth generations of immigrants who came from the same place in the Old Country — who get together for a potluck meal, games of horseshoes, and "wisiting." (See **Aal**, definition #1 and **Babel**.)

Revelation The last Book of the Bible. No one understands it, but it scares everyone anyway.

Revenge What Lutherans do to other Lutherans,

but in their hearts they know that duty belongs to God.

Reverend What you can call a pastor if you don't know his last name, as in "Here comes the Reverend." (Only dumbed-down Lutherans call a pastor by his first name, as in Pastor Doug.)

Revised Standard Version A revision of the American Standard Version of the Bible published in 1946 and 1952. Some Lutherans felt it had a Communist bent and that it didn't deliver the same punch that the King James Version did.

Revival 1. Emotionally-intense Lutheran Services that Haugeans and Free Lutherans attended. Revivals made other Lutherans nervous, especially the altar calls and the bawling and the carrying on of it. They were usually held in tents in the summer and people of other faiths attended too. 2. What a tub of wash water did to make the day lilies stand up straight. (See **Hans Nielsen Hauge**.)

Revivalist The minister in charge of a revival who usually didn't wear a suit or wear out, and who had most folks believing that they were headed straight for hell. Regular Lutherans compared him to a Holy Roller. (Even though Billy Graham wasn't a Lutheran, regular Lutherans thought he was a fine revival preacher.)

Rhubarb Sauce A sauce that wasn't usually served in the Lutheran Church, but most Lutheran women canned a lot of it.

Rhythm What Lutherans from Africa had that Norwegian-American Lutherans didn't have.

Rice Pudding What Swedes ate at Christmas instead of *rømmegrøt*.

Rickrack A decoration that was sewed on the bottom of Lutheran Church Basement aprons, 4-H style show revue dresses, and on everday dresses too. (See also **Gay**.)

Riffraff People who move into a town, don't have jobs, don't have any known relatives in the area, don't have a purpose in life, don't join a church, and just cause general chaos in a community.

Righteous A term used to describe Lutherans who do it right according to their own Biblical interpretation.

Right-Wing Lutherans who are Republican, to boot.

Rigmarole This could be anything from a girdle that doesn't fit right to a tractor seat that doesn't bounce right.

Ringer 1. The man who rings the bell for church or for the Salvation Army, and the women who get together to wear gloves and ring bells for services. 2. What men want to get in a game of horseshoes at the Annual Sunday School Picnic. (See **Gloves**.)

Rite of Passage Confirmation! When you have been confirmed you are old enough to wear nylons and lipstick, shave, date other confirmed Lutherans, and sit at the adult table on Christmas Eve.

Ritual Doing the same thing over and over even if it doesn't make sense. For instance, if a person has always sung 'Away In a Manger' one way, he certainly isn't going to acknowledge that there is another rendition. Another ritual would be to always serve *lutefisk* on Christmas Eve, even if no one at the table will eat it.

Road The road to hell is paved with good intentions. (See **Car Washes**.)

Rock and Roll A sinful form of movement which became the wreck and ruin of many a Lutheran youth. Rock and Roll got its start on the Ed Sullivan Show with Elvis Presley.

Rolling Bandages A healthy Christian service performed in the Lutheran Church Basement by The Daughters of the Reformation and by elderly

Lutheran women whose grandkids were recruited with the promise of nectar and a brownie. This was done for the good of the leper colonies and the world-at-large. (See **Leper Colony** and **Service Projects**.)

Rolls 1. A type of sweet pastry that Lutherans served between services along with coffee and nectar. (Doughnuts weren't considered rolls, but they were also served between services.) 2. What Lutheran Church Basement Women did to bandages. 3. A verb for what loose nickels would do on the church floor.

Roman Catholic Our brothers and sisters in Christ who we were taught were going to hell. (See also **Old Catholic** for the opposite view.)

Romance Novels Trashy books read in secret by some Lutheran town women.

Roman Numerals A way that ancient Romans numbered things which didn't make any sense to Lutherans.

Rook A Christian card game with no face cards. (See **Face Cards**.)

Rose of Sharon The name of some Lutheran Churches which came from a passage in the Bible that most Lutherans didn't understand.

Rosemaling The Norwegian art of painting on anything to make it prettier. Some Lutheran Church Basement bathrooms are even *rosemaled*. (See **Centennial**, *Lefse* **Turner**, and *Vesterheim*.)

Rosette A type of Scandinavian Christmas cookie that is made with lots of lard and served at *Lutefisk* suppers.

Rose Water A type of sickening perfume as pungent as lilac water that some older Lutheran ladies wore to Ladies' Aid. (See *Lefse* **Turner**.)

Roughnecks People who don't know how to act like regular Lutherans. They are a tad bit rough around the edges, and their necks don't look really clean either.

Round-the-clock This refers to care that Lutherans had to give when their relatives were doing poorly, or during calving season.

Rubberneck The act of listening in on a party-line to a conversation that was none of your business, but nevertheless important because information like births, sicknesses, and deaths could be gleaned. (See **Gossip**.)

Rubbers A type of slip-on overshoe that Lutheran men usually lost at Father-Son Banquets or at Brotherhood.

Rubbering A slang term for rubbernecking.

Rundown What happens to cemeteries if there isn't a good Cemetery Board, and how Lutheran kids get if they stay up too late memorizing.

Runner This had nothing to do with exercise, but with a white cloth placed on the aisle for brides, or a piece of *Hardangersøm* placed on the altar or the top of the piano.

Rushing Around Like a Chicken with Your Head Cut Off What Lutheran women do at Christmas time, men do during harvest, and kids do before 4-H Achievement Days.

Rust Out What happens to Lutherans who never learned how to work hard, and to black iron frying pans that aren't cleaned right.

Rutabaga A vegetable that Danish Lutherans from Askov, MN like to serve and eat.

Rye Bread The bread that Swedes thought came from heaven.

S...

Sabbath The word Early Christians used for "Sunday" as written in the King James Bible.

Sack 1. A paper bag that was filled with ribbon candy, peanuts, an apple, and chocolate haystack drops, and was given to Lutheran Sunday School children after the Christmas Program. 2. A sack made of burlap that was used for potatoes, Halloween costumes, and races at Sunday School picnics and was called a "gunny sack."

Sacraments The Christian Rites ordained by Christ which impart the means of divine grace. The Lutheran Church has two, and the Catholic Church has seven. Each church thinks it is right, and we will find out some day.

Sacrifice What Abraham and mothers do.

Sadducees A group of priests who thought they

were better than everyone else.

Saints The priesthood of all believers, according to Lutherans. Other churches had a whole list of names of saints that they had to memorize, but had no clue as to why they were saints.

Salt and Pepper 1. Lutheran Church spices. 2. A common color of hair found in the Lutheran Church Basement kitchen.

Samaritan Like every other group, there were good Samaritans and bad Samaritans, and Lutherans read a lot about them in the New Testament.

Sanctification A tough word for Confirmands to define, but invariably someone had to at Public Questioning.

Sanctuary The room in the church where general Worship Services were held and where Lutheran kids were taught that they better behave, or else!

Satan The Norwegian-American Lutheran word for the "devil."

Scald What Lutheran Church Basement Women do to the milk they put in the scalloped potatoes and ham dish that they bring to Lutheran doings.

Scandinavian Marketplace A place where Scandinavian Lutherans go to get the finest Scandinavian gifts around. Located at 218 East 2nd Street, Hastings, MN 55033, it's clean, comfortable, and loaded with merchandise.

Scarf What Lutheran women in the Midwest wore on their heads, and Lutheran kids in the snowbelt wore over their faces. (See **Kerchief.**)

Scarlet Fever A contagious disease that kept Lutheran kids from attaining perfect attendance in Sunday School.

Scarlatina A variation of scarlet fever that one could have and still go to Sunday School.

Search This used to be done to the Scriptures diligently. Now it is a word used to describe the act of looking for a church home, as in "If you are searching for a church home . . . ." (Good night then! This was never an issue before. One always knew what crossroads the church was located at. You certainly didn't have to look for it.)

Secretary The woman of the church who kept the pastor's life sorted out. She also typed the bulletins, ran the mimeograph machine, took minutes, knew shorthand, and got printer's ink all over her fingers. She usually didn't get paid much at all, but it was an honorable position.

Secular Worldly things that weren't sacred, but yet weren't all bad. For instance, John Deere Day was a secular event, but it felt sacred because the women of the church served the lunch, and it was farmers and their families who attended.

Seed Money A little starter, as in "Ole Anderson bequeathed seed money to First Lutheran so they would get on with the business of putting an elevator in the church."

Seminary Where Lutheran men went to study and learn how to be a pastor. Some were called, some followed in the family footsteps, some wanted to avoid the draft, and some went because they didn't want to own their own house and mow the lawn.

Sensible Shoes Brown or black thick-soled tie oxfords and gray Glovette wedgies.

Septuagesima A Sunday on the church calendar that no one could pronounce. Most Lutherans didn't know Greek, only Scandinavian languages or German.

Seraphim and Cherubim Angels that Lutherans sang and read about, but didn't have statues of them.

Sermon The "meat" of the services. Sometimes it is good, sometimes it is okay, and sometimes a guy can't make head nor tail out of what a pastor is trying to say. (See also **Meat**).

Sermon Notes Notes on the sermon that Confirmands were required to take. Some Confirmands didn't know how to take decent notes and were always trying to copy from the Confirmand sitting next to them.

Sermon on the Mount From Matthew, a sermon Jesus gave. Most Norwegian Lutherans thought Jesus was talking about Norwegian Lutheran farmers when he said, "Blessed are the meek, for they shall inherit the earth."

Sermonette A poor excuse for a real sermon, kind of like a kitchenette for a real kitchen.

Sermonizing What the Mrs. Snustads of the world were always doing.

Serpent A snake that tried to fool Adam and Eve

but was really the devil in disguise. Some Lutherans could be serpents, too. (See **Creation**.)

Serve What Lutheran Church Basement Women did from the time they were born until the time they died. (Some almost had to serve at their own funeral.)

Service Project Mission quilts, rolling bandages for lepers, and care kits for heathens. (See also **Leper Colony**.)

Services 1. 8:30, 9:00, 9:30, 10:00, 10:30, and 11:00. The times varied depending on how many in the congregation "milked." 2. Those who served our country were in the services. Everyone knew who they were because they always wore their uniforms to church when they were home on furlough.

Seven-Day Pickles Dark green pickles that took seven days to make, and seven seconds to eat.

Seven-Minute Frosting The good white frostings used on special birthday cakes and other special doings.

Sex Education "Men don't marry public property." 'This Is Most Certainly True!'

Shake, Rattle and Roll What was okay for Holy Rollers to do, but not Elvis Presley. (He did it anyway, even though he was a Baptist.)

Shakers 1. Containers for salt and pepper, the Lutheran spices. 2. People who lived like Lutherans, i.e., frugal and celibate, but weren't. 3. Holy Rollers.

Shame on You An oft-used phrase to keep Lutheran kids from ever believing they were better than anyone else, and to justify the odd behavior of putting scarves over their faces.

Sheath A straight, sleeveless dress that sexpots like Marilyn Monroe wore. *Nei, Fyda*! Regular Lutherans wore A-Line or gathered skirt dresses.

Sheet Music What Lutheran Churches bought without any guilt.

Shekel A denomination of money that Lutherans knew about from the Bible, but didn't know if it was worth a penny or a dime. However, parents still told their children to "save your shekels," even though the parents didn't know what a shekel was either.

Shepherds Eight or nine-year-old Lutheran boys who dressed up in worn-out bathrobes for the Annual Sunday School Christmas Program.

Shoe Horn A metal utensil that looked like a tongue. It was developed to help men get their Sunday shoes on. Confirmation age boys usually got them in a shoe kit as a Confirmation gift.

Shoo-fly What Lutheran mothers said to their children when they wanted them to get out of their way. (See **Dash**.)

Shortest Verse "Jesus wept." This is the verse that The Daughters of the Reformation recited when they were called upon to say a Bible verse and they couldn't remember any other.

Shorty Coat A type of short coat that Lutheran women wore to church in the Spring and Fall, and they were usually a tan tweed. Lutheran girls wore shorty coats for Easter. These looked and felt like cotton candy and came in colors of bubble gum pink, mint green, pale yellow, and light blue.

Shotgun Wedding The consequence Darrell and Beverly paid for not paying attention at Bible Camp.

Showers For Lutherans, showers had to do with brides and babies, and not with rain.

Shrove Tuesday The Tuesday before Ash Wednesday that Lutherans didn't observe in any Holy way.

Shrug 1. What Lutheran men do when they don't want to answer your questions. 2. A type of short shawl/sweater that Lutheran girls wore with sweater guards, and older Lutheran women wore to keep the chill off their shoulders.

Shuffleboard A clean recreational game that Lutheran youth were allowed to play in the church basement where the shuffleboard pattern was embedded right in the linoleum. (See **Games in the Basement** and **Lutheran Recreation**.)

Shut Your Eyes, Bow Your Head, and Fold Your Hands What Lutherans were taught to do when they prayed.

Sick and Tired A mental state that didn't make sense to those who were used to working, unless it was the Sunday School superintendent who was referring to the job she had for thirty years.

Silvers A shortened-up way to say "Silver Wedding Anniversaries." Silvers, as most Lutherans called them, were usually held in the church basement with programs, pourers, nuts and mints. (See **Anniversary** and **Nuts and Mints**.)

Sin (See also **Dancing**, **Chewing**, **Drinking**, **Spitting Cloves**, **Playing Cards**, **Shooting Pool**, **Necking**, and **Turning**.)

Sincerely Yours A way to sign off letters to close relatives, boyfriends and girlfriends, and others one cares deeply about. (See **Yours Truly**.)

Sinful *Rømmegrøt.*

Singing It's the same as breathing for some Lutherans, like the Nelson Family of Portland, ND.

Singspiration A songfest before something like the Mission Festival where eight hymns, like 'Bringing in the Sheaves,' were sung with vigor.

Sit Still What little Lutherans were admonished to do every Sunday.

Sitting Duck A minister who doesn't have the sense to spend enough time preparing his sermon. (See also **Lame Duck**.)

Skimpy 1. A dress that doesn't have enough material in it. 2. The amount of food served at a Lutheran funeral when there were more mourners than the Ladies Aid expected.

Skin and Bones The way a man looks if he marries a woman from town who never learned how to cook right for her man.

Skin-Tight The type of clothes worn by painted ladies and those who think they are from Hollywood.

Slang Appropriate words such as "Good Gravy!", and "Goodnight, then!"

Slipping 1. What a Lutheran woman is doing when her slip is showing below her hem line. 2. A state of mind, like when Agnes is having a tough time getting around or remembering things, one could say, "Oh, I think Agnes is slipping." 3. What Emil's car is doing when he can't control the Buick on ice. 4. What a 12-year-old Lutheran boy from North Dakota does to the clutch when he is practicing for his farm license.

Slop-Pail A galvanized pail that was used to store slop and scraps before it was dumped down the river bank, into a ditch, or given to the hogs. (The color of the outside of the slop-pail was silver gray;

the color of the scraps and slop inside the slop-pail was Pepto Bismol pink.) (See **Beet Pickles**.)

Slotted Dime Folders Cardboard folders with slots for dimes that sat on the kitchen table during Lent and were collected on Easter so the money could be used for worldwide causes.

Slow to Anger What the Sunday School superintendent wasn't the Saturday morning before the Annual Sunday School Christmas Program.

Smear What the chocolate haystack drops that children received in brown bags after the Annual Sunday School Christmas Program did to new Christmas dresses.

Smoking What some Lutheran boys did behind the barn, what happened to the coal stove when it backed up, and what some women were like when they were beyond simmering. (See **Damper**.)

Snap Outta It Lutheran psychology.

Snipe Hunt A game counselors thought up to entertain Bible Campers.

Snooze A light nap taken in church, or out on the front lawn after dinner.

Snore What Lutheran men who didn't have wives to kick them did in church when the sermon got too long and boring.

Snow Fence What Lutherans put up around cemeteries and by the entry to the church when the drifts were higher than the brooder house.

Snuff 1. Copenhagen tobacco that Scandinavian Lutheran bachelor farmers chewed. They called it *snus*. 2. A standard that women wanted their cleaning "to be up to." (See **Level-Headed** and **Straight**.)

Soap What Vacation Bible School children carved Bibles out of, what Lutheran women made for the missions, what mothers threatened to wash out little boys' mouths with, and what Lutheran farmers needed to clean up with. (See **Clean**, **Render**, **Soap**, **Squeaky Clean**, **Tallow**, **VBS**, **Washing Down**, and **Washing Up**.)

Social Problems People who lived in town and didn't own property.

Spam 1. A canned meat that had no expiration date and was embalmed in colorless gelatin. (Even though it looked like an anemic ham and could be served hot or cold, it sure didn't taste like it. Some women cheated and put it in their scalloped potatoes, but they didn't pull any wool over anyone's eyes.) Spam cans were opened by a tin key which, if it went off track, reacted like a menopausal women, i.e., it couldn't go forward, it couldn't go backward, it just dangled and was good for nothing. (However the oval cans made a good icebox cookie cutter.) 2. A newfangled word used in connection with the information age.

Spanking A form of punishment that was used in Lutheran homes when parents caught their children smoking, dancing, or playing pool and were at their wit's end.

Special Offerings Extra appeals for money that were used for the Gideons, LYE Teams, and many other groups who needed funds.

Spells What Agnes and Nellie and other Fititude ladies got when they were nervous. They usually came out of their spells though. (Years ago weak women swooned.)

Spic-and-Span 1. What the church should always look like. 2. A powdered cleaner you mix with water and use for heavy-duty housecleaning.

Spicy Foods that didn't sit well with Norwegian Lutherans.

Spikes Shoes so high they don't look Christian.

Spinster A woman who was so busy taking care of her parents and the homeplace that she didn't have time to court.

Spit Saliva that is put on a hanky to clean up a kid before he heads into church.

Split To divide. This could be a church, culottes, or the bars that were left over after a church funeral. (See **Mergers and Splits**.)

Sponsors Relatives who stood up at the Baptismal font with the parents of the baby being baptized. They usually got invited over for dinner after the Baptism, and a Lutheran child's sponsors usually gave a bigger Confirmation or wedding gift than other people did.

Spread This implies a big size and can refer to both the food on a table and how one looks after eating too much of it. It also refers to a meat concoction that was put on funeral buns. (See **Deadspreads**.)

Spritz A white cookie that is served at Christmas and at *lutefisk* suppers.

Spruce It Up What parishioners do to the graves

before Decoration Day, and to the church for the Centennial.

Sputnik A Russian satellite that went into orbit about the same time that Mrs. Snustad did when she found out the church was getting new Red Hymnals.

Squander What people do who were never taught to "Waste not, want not." (See **Basic Necessities**.)

Squeaky Clean What linoleum floors should feel like if they have been washed right, i.e., on your hands and knees with lots of soap and hot water. (See **Clean** and **Cleanse**.)

Squirm What kids in church — and women whose girdles are too tight — do.

St. Olaf Choir F. Melius's choir from Northfield, MN that sang the verses of 'Beautiful Savior' in the wrong order. (See **F. Melius** and **Order**.)

Stained Glass Windows Colorful glass that every Lutheran Church had in its sanctuary. These were usually donated "In Loving Memory Of . . ." someone by a regular. (See **Regular**.)

Stains Grass marks that little boys got on their good pants while playing tombstone tag in the cemetery, and clothing drive recipients got on their pedal pushers. (See **Pedal Pushers** and **Zululand**.)

Stale What the church smelled like when no one bothered to air it out before Sunday Services.

Standard The forerunner of 'The Lutheran Magazine.' It wasn't as controversial, either.

Standard English The kind of English that makes sense like "*Uffda, Neiman*, and Snap outta it!"

Stand Still What every Lutheran girl heard when her hair was being braided, and what every Lutheran boy heard when his pants were being hemmed up. The junior choir director also said it.

Stand Up Straight What every female Lutheran Confirmand was told to do when she was modeling her Confirmation dress and practicing walking in her Confirmation heels.

Stanley Products They weren't necessarily just Lutheran, but they cleaned like it.

Stanza A high church word for "verses," but no matter what a person called them, they were surrounded by refrains that no one knew when to sing.

Staples Salt, pepper, sugar lumps, Spam, Jell-O, Cream of Mushroom soup, and lard.

Star What Lutheran children received for attendance and memorization. They were either gold, blue or red, and came in little hard-covered boxes and the Sunday School teacher used spit on the stars to moisten the glue on the back of them.

Starving Kids in China These were the kids that Lutheran mothers talked about when their own kids balked at eating liver.

State Church The church in the Old Country that everyone couldn't wait to leave, but always tried to replicate in the new country.

Stationery Frivolous pretty paper that Lutheran children gave to their Sunday School teachers at Christmas time.

Stave Churches These were the earliest churches of Norway, and looking at the construction of them, one can't tell if heathens or Christians worshipped in them.

Steadfast Lutherans who never wavered on anything.

Steeple The top of the church that was hard to

paint and sometimes hit by lightning. A place that town people called a "bell tower," it housed both the bell and pigeons. (Most Lutherans can look at a steeple and tell you the denomination of the church.)

Step-Stool A little stool found in Lutheran Church Basements that short Lutherans had to use the reach the top shelves in the cupboards.

Stepping Out With "Courting" that is both good and bad, if you know what we mean.

Stewardship Drive A plea to the members for money. Whether it was verbal from the pulpit, or an "every member drive," it usually took place in November. (Most Lutherans preferred to figure out for themselves what they wanted to give, rather than be reminded.)

Sticky What linoleum floors in the church basement feel like when too much nectar has been spilled on them, what church pews and seven-minute frosting feels like on a humid July day, and what children's fingers feel like after they have eaten the ribbon candy they got in their Sunday School sack.

Stiletto Heels Heathen heels that made no earthly sense at all and were only worn as an attention-getter. (You rarely saw these in a Lutheran Church.) (See **Heel**, **Limp**, **Low**, **Pagan**, and **Pumps**.)

Stille Nacht The title of 'Silent Night' in German Lutheran Churches.

Stingy Someone who only makes a small hotdish and then takes more than she brought when the kitchen crew is dividing up the food. Stingy and cheap go hand-in-hand.

Stole 1. An ecclesiastical garment worn by pastors of the high church, and a fox fur worn by elderly women. (Fox furs, where the head was chasing the tail, sit in attics collecting dust now.) 2. A bad thing Herman and Melvin did to the sugar lumps in the church kitchen cupboard. (See **Lecture**.)

Stood Up For What the attendants at a wedding ceremony did. (Sensible Lutheran couples usually had only one attendant each.)

Storeroom A room in the church where the manger and the costumes for the wisemen, shepherds, angels, Mary, and Joseph were kept — along with lots of other stuff.

Stormcoat A heavy-duty coat that was the antithesis of style, but oozed with practicality.

Storyteller 1. A Sunday School teacher who was good at telling Bible stories. 2. Lutheran teenagers who stretched the truth when explaining to their parents why Luther League lasted so long.

Straight A word to describe seams and darts that were up to snuff. (See **Gay** and **Snuff**.)

Straw Wheat stalks that were dragged into church for the manger at the Annual Sunday School Christmas Program.

Substitute People who filled in for Sunday School teachers who took ill Sunday morning. (See **Ill**.)

Sugar Lumps Cubes of sugar that Norwegian Lutherans placed in their teeth and sucked coffee through, and that Norwegian Lutheran kids ate when there were no nuts and mints on the counter. (See **Lecture** and **Nuts and Mints** and **Stole**.)

Summer Services These services were usually cookers even if they started earlier in the morning than they did at other times of the year. (See **Services**.)

Sunday Drives to Look at the Fields What the men would motor around and do while the women were making a light supper. (See **Drive**.)

Sunday School The educational system set up in all Lutheran Churches to teach little Lutherans what they needed to know in life.

Sunday School Picnic An annual picnic held at the end of the Sunday School year where the pastor preached a sermonette, the kids got Dixie cups and had gunny sack races, the men snoozed and played horseshoe, and the women fixed the meal. If it rained and the picnic was held in the church base-ment, no one had any fun.

Sunday School Pin A Lutheran award given to kids who had attended Sunday School every Sun-day, even if they were sick. A first year perfect attendance award was a circle pin that had the Martin Luther symbol on it; the second year award was a wreath around the pin; and the third, fourth, etc., awards were bars that hung below the pin. Most Lutherans who received these awards still have them. 'This Is Most Certainly True!' (See **Attendance Pins.**)

Sunday School Practice This was not to practice Sunday School, but rather to practice the Annual Christmas Program, and these were held for many Saturday mornings before the actual program.

Sunday School Program Baby Jesus, Mary, Joseph, 'Away in a Manger,' shepherds, wisemen, angels, pieces, 'Silent Night,' new clothes, Christmas trees, ribbon candy, peanuts, apples, and chocolate haystack drops. Some kids yelled, "Hi, Mommy!", some sang off-key, some forgot their pieces, and some had to go potty.

Sunday School Superintendent A woman who had the second highest calling in the Lutheran Church Basement, right below the Ladies Aid President. (Normally a Sunday School superintendent was a "take charge" woman who only got ruffled and threatened to quit the whole blasted works the Saturday before the Annual Sunday School Christmas Program.)

Sunshine Club A group of Lutheran women who had some extra time on their hands and made sure everyone got a card or some cheer when they needed it. (See **Club** and **Homebound**.)

Support Group A group of people who have the same problem and meet together to help each other cope. (These groups came into vogue about the same time the Green Hymnal did. Before that everyone just kept it to themselves.)

Swear A Revised Standard Version way of saying "curse."

Sweat What the workers at *Lutefisk* suppers did,

especially those who both "mashed" and suffered from hotflashes.

Sweltering What a small Lutheran Church sanctuary felt like in the middle of July at the 10:00 Services when no air was moving.

Swenson Brothers Bachelor farmers from Flom, MN who are good with wood and eat *lutefisk*.

Synod ALC, ELC, LFC, LCA, AALC, EFCA, TALC, LCMS, AFLC, ULCA, WELS, ELS, ELCA etc., etc., etc.

T...

Tabasco A runny hot tomatoey concoction that comes in a jar that looks similar to a Lucky Tiger Hair Oil jar, only smaller. Because most Lutheran recipes don't call for Tabasco Sauce, Lutheran women usually have no idea why they bought it, but they do know that one jar will last a lifetime.

Tabloid 1. A modern name for the church annual report. 2. Issues of the 'National Geographic' that had photographs of bare-naked tribal people in it. (See **Naked** and **Pickles**.)

Tablecloths Big rectangular pieces of cotton, oil, damask, netting, and lace that were used for table coverings in the Lutheran Church Basement.

Tacky 1. Cheap showiness characterized by a lack of decent breeding and common sense. 2. The way a newly varnished church pew felt on a Lutheran lady's amply-proportioned legs as she tried to "unglue" her legs, hose, and Orlon dress when she had to stand up for the reading during a muggy, summer Sunday Morning Service. 3. A word for the spot on the linoleum floor under the nectar and/or lemonade table, heard especially during the era of rubber-soled wedgies, i.e., 1956-1959.

Taco A counterfeit version of *lefse* rolled up and stuffed with lettuce, tomato, ground beef, and spices that would give most Scandinavian Lutherans a good case of indigestion. Pronounced "tack-o" in some Scandinavian Lutheran hinterlands.

Talcum Powder A perfumed dusting powder often given to a Sunday School teacher for a Christmas present, and usually bought at the local drugstore or from the Avon lady. It was also used to keep "flats" smelling fresh when they were worn without nylons at Evening Services at Bible Camp, and as a type of play makeup for the face and hair that made youngsters look as old as Moses or like they had leprosy. (See **Pump Organ Shoes** and **Leper Colony**.)

Tallow The white, solid, rendered fat of butchered livestock that was used for making homemade lye mission soap and candles, and for rubdowns on a person who had a puzzling skin rash or whatever stuff was going around. (See **Lard**, **Liniment**, and **Carbo-Salve**.)

Tambourine A small hand drum played at the Mission Festival by foreign missionaries for Show and Tell. Even though the Bible speaks of tambourines, Martin Luther never considered using such in the hymns he wrote.

Tangles 1. A noun for the knots in children's permed hair that had to be brushed out before Sunday School, and for knots that occurred in the yarn when Gladys wasn't paying attention while she was crocheting doilies for the Fall bazaar. 2. A verb for the mess Gloria Jean got into when she started to fall for a good-for-nothing town boy. (See **Frizzy** and **Perm**.)

Tattered To become worn and ragged from neglect, such as a Norwegian bachelor farmer's flannel shirt which was seldom washed and never mended, but still worn to *lutefisk* suppers.

Tattoo An indelible often lewd or heathenish mark that people with no thought to the consequences or turmoil they'd create, had branded onto their arm or chest. Military men sometimes had a flag or the word, "Mom," tattooed on their arms, but that was different.

Temperance Union A group of no-nonsense women who started an organization to keep the town dry, the men in line, and the children on the straight and narrow. Joining this group was as political as most Scandinavian Lutheran women ever got.

Temptation The act of a Catholic enticing a Lutheran to do something sinful like dancing, and the act of a Lutheran enticing a Catholic to eat a hot dog on Friday.

Ten Commandments The "Thou shalt nots . . ." given to Moses on Mt. Sinai. Martin Luther, the German, wrote meanings to the Ten Commandments so Lutheran Confirmands would learn how to memorize.

Ten O'clock Worship Services The time that most country Lutheran Churches started their Summer Worship Services. In the winter services began at 11:00 o'clock because of the weather and shoveling and everything.

Ten Social Commandments The "Thou shalt nots . . ." commanded by Norwegian Lutheran pastors who weren't even close relatives of Moses. Examples of the Social Commandments include: Thou shalt not dance; Thou shalt not go to movies; and Thou shalt not date outside the faith, i.e., Thou shalt not do anything fun. (See also page 57 in the book, 'Growing Up Lutheran.')

Tenor 1. A potential baritone who hasn't shaved or been confirmed yet. 2. A lazy alto. (See **Alto**.)

Tent 1. A temporary covering for outdoor revival meetings which were held in the summer. (Baptists felt more comfortable sitting in a tent for church than did Lutherans.) 2. A dress style that was in vogue in the early 60s, and worn by town and country women who had a "bun in the oven."

Thankful Even though "thankful" literally means to be conscious of benefits already received, Norwegian Lutherans were admonished to be thankful always, whether there were benefits or not. The logic was that no matter how bad it got, there were always others who had it worse, i.e., "Just be thankful you have liver and *gammelost* to eat. Think of all the starving kids in China!"

Thanksgiving A national holiday that Lutherans celebrated pretty much the same as other people in the United States, except that Norwegian Lutherans always went to church, served *lefse*, and certainly didn't buy any foods at a "deli" for Thanksgiving. Everything from the pickles to the pumpkin pie was homemade.

Therapy Whether one had a bodily, mental, or behavioral disorder, the best therapy was to go do the barn chores.

Thermal Underwear Heavy-duty underwear that was only worn to church when it was beastly *kaldt*. (See **Beastly Cold**.)

This is Most Certainly True You couldn't get confirmed in the Lutheran Church if you didn't know what this meant! 'This Is Most Certainly True!'

"Thrash" This is a Scandinavian-Lutheran word that stems from the English word, "trash," referring to slinky women at a carnival whose earrings are bigger than their pants.

Throne 1. A Lutheran way to refer to the toilet. 2. The chair that the pastor sat in when the choir was singing.

Tie A thin piece of silk fabric that was knotted at the neck and worn to church. Lutherans younger than Confirmation age sometimes wore bow ties, but after they were confirmed, they wore regular ties. Most Lutheran men received enough ties for Christmas and Father's Day to last them for more than a lifetime.

Tithing The act of giving the first fruits, i.e., one-tenth of what one makes, to church. It was good in theory, but apparently not practiced by everyone, considering all the bazaars that Lutheran

Churches had to have in order to keep the coffers going. Some even considered the ham they gave to the pastor at Christmas as part of their tithe.

To Turn 1. When a Lutheran was engaged to a Catholic, everyone asked, "I wonder which one is going 'to turn?'" Some "turned" just to keep peace with one side of the family which, in turn, upset the other side of the family. 2. "To turn" was also used in reference to *lefse*, such as "You're going to have to turn that *lefse* quick, Gloria Jean, or it will be too tough to eat." (See *Lefse* **Turner**.)

Toilet Water Perfumes like lilac water that stunk like toilet water. (See also **Rose Water**.)

Toivo and Eino Only Finnish Lutherans named their kids Toivo and Eino. If you were Norwegian Lutheran, you named your kids sensible names like Ola and Per, but sometimes called them names like Slim and Spud.

Tombstone Tag A running tag game that creative, bored Lutheran country kids played in the adjoining church cemetery to pass time when their parents were "wisiting" and drinking coffee in the church basement. Daring Lutheran boys often jumped the tombstones in order to make the game more exciting.

Tour What Lutheran college choirs did every year throughout the Midwest, and once in a blue moon to Europe.

Towels White cotton squares that had their own special drawers in Lutheran Church Basement kitchens. The women took turns taking the dirty towels home to wash, especially if they had a load of diapers to do anyway.

Town Women A phrase used by country women to describe women who lived in town. Lutheran town women took shortcuts and brought store-bought bread and cakes from the bakery to church without any shame at all. They dressed differently, too. Some even played canasta in front of their picture windows without even drawing the drapes.

Tracts Thought-provoking pamphlets on various topics published by Augsburg Publishing House that were placed in a rack at the back of the church or in the back of the church basement's general lunch area. These tracts were nonthreatening ways for Lutherans to evangelize. The theory behind tracts was that someone who really needed help could gain some insight from a tract and not have to bother the pastor with their problems.

Tract Rack A varnished rack that held tracts. It usually was missing a nail in a strategic place, thus messing up some of the tracts.

Train 1. The mode of transportation that most Luther Leaguers took to get to their national conventions. 2. An attachment on a bride's gown that sometimes tripped her up. 3. Train Up A Child . . . . A Bible verse that most Lutherans believe justified memorization, and tripped some of them up, too.

Training Grounds Sunday School, Confirmation, Bible School, Bible Camp, Luther League, Lutheran Bible Schools, and Lutheran Colleges before 1962.

Tramp A transient hobo who jumped off the train in a small rural community and without any pride or shame went to the Lutheran Church or a farm house to beg for food or money.

Treasurer The keeper of the purse strings. Because of all their fundraisers, the Ladies Aid treasurer had to keep her facts and figures straight, that was for sure then!

Treats Bags containing ribbon candy, peanuts, chocolate haystack drops, and one apple or orange that were given to Sunday School kids after the Christmas program.

Tribe 1. Joseph's sons each had their own tribe, and Lutheran Confirmands had to memorize all 12 tribe's names. 2. What Lutheran families who had as many kids as Catholic families did were said to have.

Trinity 1. The name given the Triune God. 2. A common name for a Lutheran Church. 3. Part of the church year that didn't have any pageantry or programs in it.

Triple Trio A collection of nine women who sang at various functions in the church. Some sang soprano, some sang alto, some sang "second," and some couldn't sing very well at all, but no one cared because they were all willing to practice and perform.

Tug-of-War A game played at Bible Camp. The girls were on one end of a rope and the boys were on the other end, and the object of the game was to pull the other side through something like a mud puddle. The boys always won, but back in the 50s girls thought that was the way it should be.

Turn for the Worse A phrase used to describe someone who was slipping fast, i.e., "Nellie took a turn for the worse." (See **Slipping**.)

Twine A strong twisted string used as a belt for shepherds in the Christmas program, and for holding together the haybales that were used in the Christmas program manger.

Two-Timers 1. Lutherans who attended church twice a year, Christmas and Easter. 2. Those who broke the commandments and went out catting with another man's wife. (Women who did this weren't two-timers; they were sluts.)

U...

Ukulele An instrument not sanctioned for the sanctuary, but okay at a hootenanny or at Bible Camp. (See **Jam**.)

Ultramodern A word used to describe Lutheran Churches that were built in the 60s by architects who convinced Lutherans that the tried and true designs weren't good enough in the new day and age. Most real Lutherans thought newfangled churches looked odd, felt cold, and they didn't like the A-line roofs.

Uncivilized Heathens from other countries who didn't wear a whole lot of clothes, went barefoot in public, and danced to drums.

Unclean A word originally referring to the lepers in the Bible, but Lutheran Church Basement Women thought it meant anyone who didn't clean up good before he came to church. (See **Neck Ring**.)

Uncomfortable The way some Lutherans felt when they were told to shake hands with total strangers in church. (See **Peace**.)

Union Suit A type of jumpsuit that Lutheran farmers wore under their clothes when it was cold. Like cellars, these also had trap doors. (See **Beastly *Kaldt*.**)

Unison In the Lutheran Church this had to do with singing, not with being of one accord. (See **Mergers and Splits**.)

United 1. The name of many Lutheran Churches in America. 2. What the mergers try to accomplish but never fully succeed in doing.

Unorthodox Anything that isn't done in the old normal Lutheran way.

Unstable 1. The way some Lutheran women acted when they were going through difficulties that they didn't dare talk about to anyone. (See **Tracts**.) 2. The way some church basement chairs felt to hefty Lutherans. (See **Lard**.)

Uppity An air of superiority that town women and some pastors' wives displayed.

Upright Piano The style of piano found in the basement of the church, but not in most sanctuaries. Sometimes there was an upright in the balcony, but most people couldn't see it. (See **Organ** and **Pumps**.)

Upstairs to the Sanctuary Where Lutherans were sent to sing hymns while they waited for their ticket number to be called so they could go downstairs for the *Lutefisk* supper.

Usher 1. A Lutheran man who escorts Lutherans to their regular pews, helps take the offering, lights the altar candles, keeps the communion line going in the right direction, straightens up the hymnals after the services, and carries out unstable women who have had a spell. There are head ushers, regular ushers, and usher committees. They aren't as organized as the Ladies Aid, but they get the job done. 2. What all Lutherans do at church on New Year's Eve, i.e., they usher in the new year (at church.)

V...

VBS 1. Abbreviation and common name for Vacation Bible School which was a church school held in the summer where Lutheran children memorized, had long recesses, carved Holy Bibles out of Ivory soap, and made crosses out of cork. 2. Initials that were fingernail-polished on Mrs. Snustad's daughter's cakepan that stood for Valerie Borghild Snustad.

Veil Pieces of netting that covered the faces of Lutheran brides and the eyes of proper Lutheran women who wore hats. (See **Train**.)

Velvet 1. An expensive red or blue material that was used for making Sunday School Christmas dresses and was often cut wrong on the nap. 2. A kind of tobacco that German Lutheran pastors smoked in pipes, as in, "Mrs., I need to bring another can of Red Velvet to the sacristy." (Some say that some German Lutheran pastors even drank beer once in a while.)

Vending Machine An upright machine that dispenses Coca Cola, Nesbitt's orange, grape, and yellow pop, and was put near the shuffleboard court in Lutheran youth rooms in the late 60s to try keep the teens in church and out of the pool halls, bowling alleys, and dance halls. (See **Contemporary** and **Pool Hall**.)

Vesterheim 1. A museum in Decorah, IA that collects Norwegian immigrant church buildings, *rosemaled* things, and just about anything else that is decent and in good shape that Norwegian Lutherans will donate in loving memory. 2. Just like Kristin Lavransdatter took a pilgrimage to Trondheim, Norwegian Lutherans take pilgrimages to *Vesterheim*, their Vatican in Decorah, and try to pay their homage in July during Nordic Fest.

Vestibule The area of the church where men hung up their stormcoats and took off their rubbers and hats. It was also a place for tract racks, shaking the pastor's hand after services, and staging a final viewing area for departed Lutherans in caskets.

Vestments Garb worn by Lutheran ministers of the high church persuasion. (<u>Don't</u> see **Freer** or **Hans Nielsen Hauge**.)

Verily, Verily Biblical repetitious words that

always preceded, "I Say Unto You," which got little Lutherans to sit up straight and pay attention.

Vice 1. A frowned upon activity like dancing or card-playing. (See **Rook**.) 2. A tool (usually spelled "vise," but it sounds like "vice") used to clamp recently glued pews together that had split due to age, dry weather, and hefty Lutherans.

Victory 1. When a congregation votes to change hymnals. 2. When a congregation votes to keep hymnals.

Viewpoint There are many different viewpoints about which hymnal Lutherans should use. 'This Is Most Certainly True!'

Vigil To hold out on getting a new hymnal, i.e., "to sit vigil."

Vigilantes A group of Lutheran holdouts that won't go along with the new hymnal.

Vikings A group of Norwegians who plundered, pillaged, and acted like a bunch of heathens because they weren't confirmed. *Mange tusen takk* to St. Olaf for getting the Vikings "to turn" and settle down to fish, farm, and eat lunch like normal Lutherans. (Some of this pagan Viking behavior has been passed down through the generations and manifests itself at the Annual Congregational Meetings.)

Vision 1. A nonthreatening way for a pastor to introduce to the congregation the idea that it is time to have a building program, i.e., "I have a vision for this congregation that needs your support and prayer." 2. What some emotional Lutherans see when they go into a trancelike state. (Haybelly Hanson says is all in their heads.)

Visit (Also pronounced "Wisit" in places like Middle River, MN and Westby, WI.) 1. A Sunday afternoon Lutheran family's outing to go see another Lutheran family where the men sit and twiddle their thumbs, take a light snooze, go look at the fields, and eat lunch; the women exchange recipes, butter buns, whip the cream for the Jell-O, and cut the cake for the lunch; and the kids tear around the house jumping on beds and hiding in closets, swing on the rope in the haybarn, and ride the rusty stanchions like they're horses until lunch is served. Then, like heathens, the kids tear the crusts and globs of hard butter off the cold, roast beef sandwiches while laughing and spilling Watkin's Orange Nectar all over the one-day-old washed and waxed kitchen linoleum floor. This scenario is called a visit, or a "wisit." 2. A Christian way to announce you are going to go to the bathroom, as in "I have to visit Mrs. Jones, then."

3. To go to the cemetery, as in "I am going to visit the graves today to fix them up for Decoration Day." (See **Decoration Day** and **Remembrance Day**.)

Visitation 1. A respectful act of showing up at Olson's Funeral Parlor to view the body of a departed Lutheran, see who gave the biggest bouquets of glads and mums, check to see if the Olson's did a good job on him, sign the guestbook, and pray you don't run into any of the departed's family before you get out of there. Coffee and cookies are not part of this type of Lutheran visitation. (See **Pay Respect**.) 2. When it's time to build a new parish education building or do some extensive remodeling to the sanctuary, certain members are called upon to go on an "every member visitation" to get $1,000 from Ole Axelson, $500 from Hjalmer Johnson, $500 from Wally Olson, and any other honest donations they can pretty well count on from the others.

Visiting 1. A pastor who fills in for another pastor's annual Sunday off, as in "That visiting pastor sure can preach better than the one we have." 2. A duty the Sunshine Club does to cheer up a member who at one time worked hard in the church, but who now is doing poorly and can't get around like she used to do. 3. "Visiting the iniquities upon the third and fourth generations" explained to Lutherans why the apple didn't fall far from the tree, as in "I knew that kid's grandpa, and he sure was a bad apple too."

Visitor A person who attends a Lutheran Church away from home and gets all uneasy when the Baptist-acting Lutheran minister announces from his pulpit, "If we have any visitors here today, please raise your hand." (See **Peace**.)

Volumes The amount of material that Lutheran Confirmands had to memorize.

Volunteers This is the gas in the engine of the Lutheran Church.

Värmland An area in Sweden that lost an awful lot of skinny Swedish Lutheran farmers to emigration.

Værsågod A Norwegian Lutheran word that meant, "Come and eat now before it gets too cold, then."

W...

Waitress A girl who was chosen by a bride to clear dishes, refill coffee cups, and pass out cake at a wedding. Usually a waitress was a pretty good friend of the bride, but not as good a friend as an attendant.

Walther, C.F.W. The German Lutheran pope.

Walther League Named after the German Lutheran quasi-pope, Reverend C.F.W. Walther, Walther League was the youth group that German Lutheran teens attended. It was similar to Luther League, but Walther League kids went to different youth conventions and different Bible Camps than Luther Leaguers. Walther Leaguers couldn't go to baccalaureate and Luther Leaguers had to be there. However, some Walther Leaguers were even allowed to dance. 'This Is Most Certainly True!'

Wand A skinny blonde stick that some frail, anemic-looking junior choir directors repetitively tapped on the top of a music stand to get Lutheran juniors to pay attention.

War Paint A slang word for "makeup" that is so thick you can actually see it on someone's face. *Fyda!*

"Warsh" A German or Scandinavian immigrant's pronunciation of "wash." (See **Clean**.)

Wash-and-Wear A term used to describe clothes that didn't need to be sprinkled or ironed. Fabrics such as Banlon or Orlon fit into this category, and freed up a woman's Tuesdays.

Washing Down The act of scrubbing walls, cream separators, cupboards, dirty kids, or anything else with heavy-duty soap and heavy-duty action. Washing Down was always part of housecleaning.

Washing Up 1. This is the act of washing (with warm water and Lava Soap) the face, front and back of the neck, and hands and arms up to the elbows in an enameled wash bowl, usually in the basement or on the porch. It was done by men before dinner time if they had been out in the fields or in the barn. Women didn't wash up because they had their hands in soapy water all day anyway. Bachelor farmers who normally didn't bathe more than a couple times a year would usually wash up before they went to town Saturday night or to the Annual *Lutefisk* Supper. 2. A phrase a woman uses when she is talking about cleaning the dishes. For example, one would say, "Hurry up and wash up those dishes before someone comes."

Watch Night A Midnight Devotional Service held on New Year's Eve that faithful Lutherans attended rather than the VFW dance. The pastor preached, the women served lunch, the men yawned, and the kids rang the bell. (See **Usher**, definition #2.)

Watered Down A term used to describe a sermon that didn't have any meat, hell, or fire and brimstone in it. "Watered down" sermons got Lutherans to feel guilty about not feeling guilty.

Watkins Household foods, medicines, and cleaning products sold by a door-to-door salesman. Lutheran farm women usually bought nectar and vanilla for cooking, Carbo-salve for medicine, and some cleaning products if they couldn't say no.

Wedgie A casual, sensible, comfortable shoe (usually in a gray, black, or white color) that Lutheran women wore when serving in the Lutheran Church. Even though wedgies had a heel and were open-toed, they weren't considered provocative or worldly because the heels were thick and white anklets were worn with them. (See **Funeral Shoes**.)

Wednesday Night The night of the week that was designated church night after the Red Hymnal came into use. Normally Lutherans didn't have Wednesday Night Services unless it was Lent. Wednesday night was a night for Leagues, Choir Practices, etc.

What Does This Mean? The question the pastor asked Lutheran kids who were reciting the meanings of 'Luther's Small Catechism.' (See also **How Is This Done?** and **This Is Most Certainly True**.)

Whipped Cream Thick creamery cream that would whip easy. It was used as a topping for Jell-0, fruit soup, and or angel food cake. (See **White**.)

Whippersnapper A term old Lutheran men used when speaking about young Lutheran men who were making spendy, foolish church decisions when they were still wet behind the ears.

Whiskbroom A baby broom that was used to sweep crumbs off the oil cloth before one took a dishrag to it.

White The color of Scandinavian Lutheran foods that made these folks feel comfortable; foods such as *lutefisk, lefse,* mashed potatoes, *rømmegrøt,* cream on bread, sugar cookies, and lard.

Whither Thou Goest A phrase from the 'Book of Ruth' that became a song that was sung at Lutheran weddings. Lutheran farm brides knew that this meant that they would be following their husband to the homeplace, following him to the barn when he needed help, following him out to the field with the "Termos" and dinner, and following him around Machinery Hill at the State Fair, and all without complaining.

Wholesome A good Lutheran term used to describe people, places, and things that are decent.

Widow One-fourth of the population of most Lutheran Churches, and one-half of the population of the Ladies Aid. Widows usually had a lot of time on their hands and could always be counted on for showing up at funerals of deceased members that didn't have any known relatives in the area, and at Public Questioning even if they didn't know any of the Confirmands.

Wiggle More than a squirm, it was a description of a lewd walk used by young wayward Lutheran women who, for some reason or another, needed to get attention. As Mrs. E.A. Snustad, Ladies Aid President Emeritus of Trinity Free Lutheran of Hector, MN said to the pastor, "There they were, wiggling down the street in tight skirts dressed like streetwalkers, looking like painted ladies, and skipping junior choir practice, to boot." *Nei Fyda!* (See **Lewd**.)

Wiggling Out of a Good Girdle The unLutheran-looking actions of pulling, tugging, and huffing performed every Sunday by Lutheran women as they tried to peel off their good girdles.

Wine An alcoholic drink that Lutherans used only at Communion, but not at weddings like they did in the Bible.

Wintering Corpses A term used to describe the act of stacking caskets filled with deceased Lutherans in a holding area such as a granary until the ground thawed.

Wisemen Three young Lutheran boys who are selected and coerced to play the role of the Biblical wisemen in the Annual Sunday School Christmas Program. Usually they wear old choir robes and crowns of tin foil and carry wrapped Christmas boxes that are supposed to contain gold, frankincense, and myrrh. (See **Nativity**.)

Worcestershire Sauce A hard-to-pronounce vinegary spice concoction that someone snuck in as a legitimate ingredient in some barbecue recipes in Lutheran Church cookbooks. Most Lutheran cooks knew their people didn't like foreign smells and spices so they never used it and substituted water in its place. (See **Tabasco** and **Recipe**.)

Work A Norwegian Lutheran activity of the body, mind, and soul that defines who we are, what we do, and where we are going in life.

Worked Up Lutherans who were agitated to the point that they couldn't work as hard as they should. Mergers, new hymnals, and pastors' wives who didn't go to Ladies Aid or wore pedal pushers downtown where men and everyone could see them were things that worked up Lutherans.

Working Woman Usually a greedy woman who works outside the home so she can have more material things in life. Consequently, she is the one who is too busy to teach Sunday School, and the one who uses a cake mix to bring to a funeral. It catches up with her though. It always does.

Wormwood and the Gall Words in a Lutheran hymn that everyone sang, but didn't understand. You tell me and we will both know. (See **Gall**.)

Worry Wart Lutheran Church Basement Women who are always concerned that there isn't going to be enough food to go around, no matter what the occasion.

Worthy To be meritorious or worthy of anything is not a Lutheran way to think. It smacks of pride and pretense. If a Lutheran is honored or happens to get an award, it is thought of as luck, not worth. (See **Cakewalk**.)

Wrap up A term that has to do with leftovers, hotdishes in dishtowels, Cemetery Board meetings, and post-menopausal older women who get chilled fast.

Xmas A non-Lutheran way to spell Christmas. Most Lutherans feel guilty shortening up the spelling of Christmas even though the "X" is a symbol for Christ.

X-ray Machine A machine that Lutheran children used to put their feet into at the shoestore to get measured for new Christmas or Easter shoes.

Xylophone A percussion instrument that was played in the high school band, but not in church, at least not in small rural Lutheran ones.

Y...

Yam 1. A town name for a sweet potato. This vegetable was usually never served in the Lutheran Church, and was about as popular as a turnip. 2. "Yam" was an acceptable pronunciation for a fruit spread that was put on toast, i.e., "Please pass the 'yellie and yam'."

Yawn A term used to describe an automatic reflex that happens in church when the sermon is too long and not threatening enough.

Ye Often preceded by "Go."

Yeast 1. The ingredient in bread that drove new Lutheran brides to tears and to volunteer to bring banana bread. 2. An infection that Lutheran women would read about in the "doctor book" but they sure wouldn't ever tell their husbands or their good female Lutheran friends that they might have it because it seemed like only heathens could get it. 3. An ingredient that non-Lutherans mixed with barley to make devil's drink. (See **Jail**.)

Yellow 1. The color of the largest Pyrex bowl that Lutheran women used when they were asked to bring a big batch of scalloped potatoes and ham or a hamburger-noodle hotdish for a doings or funeral. (The other bowls — in descending size order — were green, red, and blue.) 2. An acceptable pronunciation for Jell-O from those who just came over from the Old Country.

Ylvisaker, John A contemporary Bach whose music got stiff Black Hymnal Lutherans drifting away from '*Landstad's Psalmebog*' to the point that they were almost swaying and clapping in front of others, not just at Bible Camp, but at the 10:00 o'clock Services too. (See **Contemporary**.)

YMCA A decent place where young Lutheran men stayed (unless they had an aunt to stay with) when they went to the big city.

Yoke 1. The Norwegian Lutheran pronunciation of "Joke." 2. Oppressive burdens that conscientious Lutherans felt they had to shoulder in order to be better Christians. These burdens included finding out that the 17-year-old Swenson Girl was p.g., and you — her fourth grade Sunday School teacher — probably could have prevented this by making her do more memory work in Sunday School. (See **Bear/Bore** and **Burdens**.)

Yonder Even though the word, "yonder" is found in hymns such as 'When The Roll is Called Up Yonder,' Norwegian Lutherans don't really use this word to describe a place you can't see because it doesn't make any sense to them. An antonym to "yonder" would be the North Forty, a word that has some direction to it.

Young Seminarian A term used for a young man who was studying for the ministry. He was at the seminary because he was called, wanted to avoid the draft, or his grandfather and father were ministers and he knew he was expected to be one, too. Young Seminarians usually had "pie-in-the-sky" dreams of making major changes in the church, but these were usually squelched the first week at their first call, or they sure didn't last long.

Young Seminarian's Wife The wife of a young seminarian. She usually didn't make many brownie points because she did things like use rubber gloves when she was washing dishes in the church basement. However, when she became a real pastor's wife, she wouldn't be washing dishes in the church basement so there wouldn't be any problem. (See **Half-Hearted**.)

Yours Truly A sensible, nonthreatening Lutheran way to sign a letter to someone close to you, like your betrothed. (See **Sincerely Yours**.)

Youth Group Organizations in the Lutheran Church that included Luther League, Walther League, Sewing Club, The Daughters of the Reformation, Young People's Societies, and various Missionary Societies. These organizations were started to provide good, fun, wholesome Christian fellowship for Lutheran youth. Activities at youth groups included shuffleboard, Wink 'em, blowing marshmallows across the table, hayrides, and anything else decent that would keep Lutheran youth from dancing. (See **Activities** and **Good Reading Material**.)

Yule Another name for Christmas that Norwegian Lutherans pronounce "Yule," but spell *Jul.*

Yust vent litt Part Norwegian and part Norwegian-American.

YWCA A safe place where young Lutheran women from the farm stayed when they, for one reason or another, convinced their parents that they had to go to a big city such as Minneapolis.

Z...

Zaccheus A New
Testament figure who,
like many a Lutheran
woman, was up
a tree because company
was coming to visit.

Zebra 1. An animal that was dressed like a nun
and showed up in missionaries' slides. 2. The
largest size bra in a German Lutheran Church
Basement kitchen.

Zero Hour A time of reckoning. For Lutherans,
Zero Hour occurred at Catechization. (See also
Public Questioning.)

Zeta House This on-campus house at Augsburg
College was home to 13 Lutheran girls who were
supposed to be preparing themselves to be "educated for service," but they often got distracted, and

it wasn't by dust either. (See **Iota House**.)

Zucchini Bread A sweet bread which was never eaten in the Lutheran Church Basement, only sold in the basement at the annual bazaar. Most Lutherans didn't even know what zucchini was until the Green Hymnal was introduced. Before that, Lutheran women only made banana, date, or pumpkin breads.

Zululand A country in Africa where those who were converted received used pedal pushers with beet and chokecherry stains on them from the Lutheran Women's Clothing Drive. (See **Pedal Pushers**.)

ABBREVIATIONS USED
IN THIS DICTIONARY

AAL   Aid Association for Lutherans
AALC   American Association of Lutheran Churches
AFLC   Association of Free Lutheran Congregations
ALC   American Lutheran Church
EFCA   Evangelical Free Church of America
ELC   Evangelical Lutheran Church
ELCA   Evangelical Lutheran Church in America
ELS   Evangelical Lutheran Synod
FFA   Future Farmers of America
K.P.   Kitchen Patrol
LB   Lutheran Brotherhood
LBI   Lutheran Bible Institute
LCA   Lutheran Church of America
LFC   Lutheran Free Church
LCMS   Lutheran Church—Missouri Synod
LYE   Lutheran Youth Encounter
(P.T.) Past Tense
P.G.   Pregnant
P.A.   Public Address
P.K.   Preacher's Kid
REA   Rural Electric Association
TALC   The American Lutheran Church
ULCA   United Lutheran Churches of America
WELS   Wisconsin Evangelical Lutheran Synod
VFW   Veterans of Foreign Wars
VBS   Vacation Bible School

ORDER FORM

LUTHER'S SMALL DICTIONARY

Name_____

Address_____

City_____ State_____ Zip_____

No. of copies ____@ $9.95   Subtotal $ _____

PLUS Postage & Handling:
    1st Class: $3.50 / book   or
    Book Rate: $2.50 / book $_____

    MN Residents add 6.5% Sales tax $_____

                        TOTAL $_____

Send check or money order to:

    CARAGANA PRESS
    P.O. Box 396
    Hastings, MN 55033

Or Call (800) 950-6898 or (800) 494-9124